# Bob Spain's Canoeing Guide and Favorite Texas Paddling Trails



River Books
Sponsored by
The Meadows Center for Water and the Environment
Texas State University

Texas State University
Andrew Sansom, *General Editor*

BOB SPAIN

*Foreword by* ANDREW SANSOM

*Illustrations by* JOY EMSHOFF

*Maps by* JOSHUA BAILEY

# Bob Spain's Canoeing Guide and Favorite Texas Paddling Trails

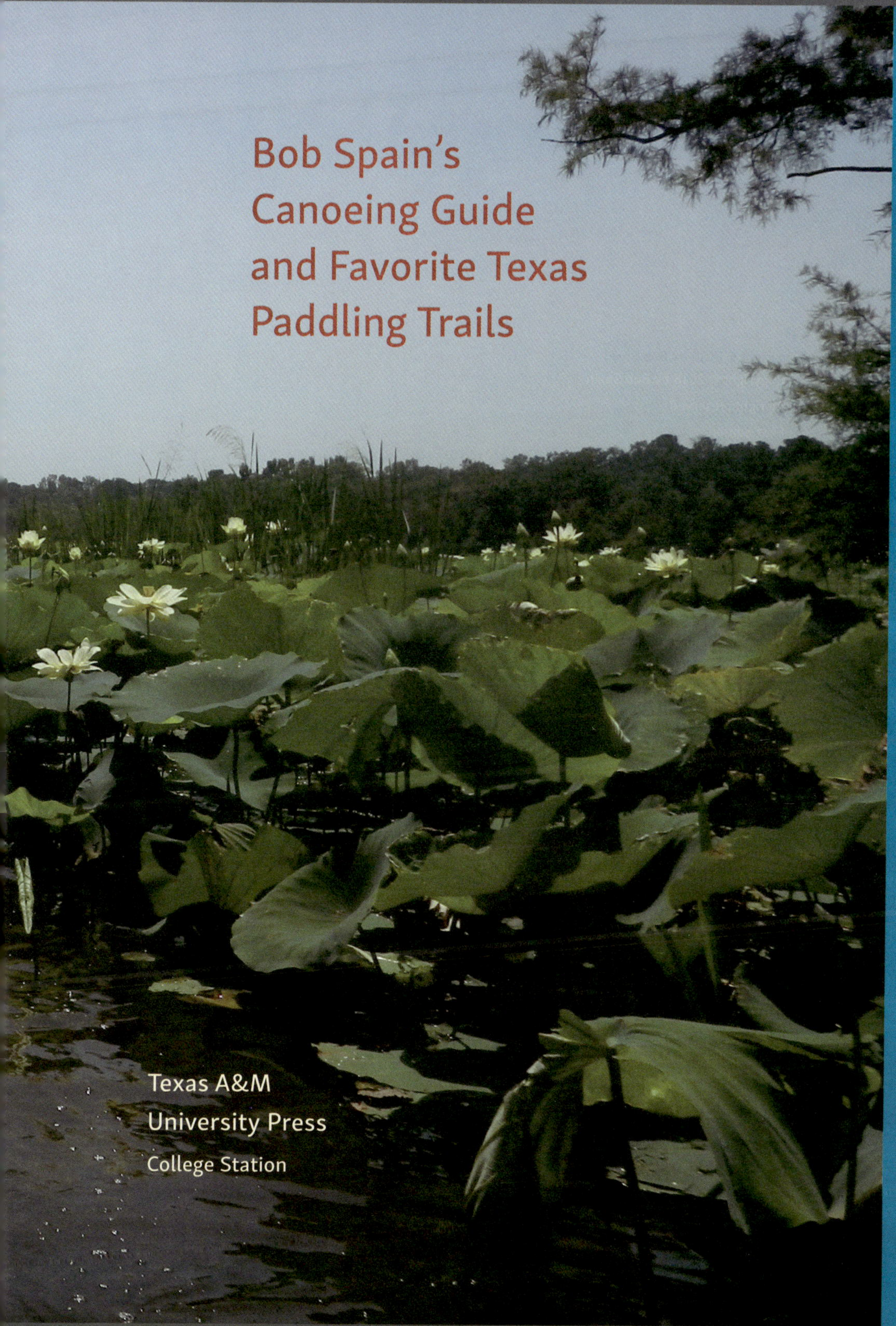

Texas A&M
University Press
College Station

First edition

This paper meets the requirements of ANSI/NISO Z39.48-1992 (Permanence of Paper).
Binding materials have been chosen for durability.
Manufactured in China through Four Color Print Group.
∞

Library of Congress Cataloging-in-Publication Data
Names: Spain, Bob, author.
Title: Bob Spain's canoeing guide and favorite Texas paddling trails / Bob Spain ; illustrations by Joy Emshoff ; maps by Joshua Bailey.
Other titles: Canoeing guide and favorite Texas paddling trails | River books (Series)
Description: First edition. | College Station : Texas A&M University Press, [2018] | Series: River books | Includes bibliographical references and index.
Identifiers: LCCN 2017035289| ISBN 9781623496180 (paper (with flaps) : alk. paper) | ISBN 9781623496197 (e-book)
Subjects: LCSH: Canoes and canoeing—Texas—Guidebooks | Water trails—Texas—Guidebooks
Classification: LCC GV776.T4 S73 2018 | DDC 797.12209747—dc23 LC record available at https://lccn.loc.gov/2017035289—

*A list of titles in this series is available at the end of the book.*

# Contents

# Contents

# Foreword

More years ago than I would like to admit, when I was working at the Texas Parks and Wildlife Department, the general manager of the Lower Colorado River Authority challenged me to a canoe race on the river below Austin. I called my colleague Bob Spain, who worked in the building with me, and asked him to join me in the stern of my old canoe. When we got in the water Bob instructed me to do only what he told me and that he would take care of the rest. When the starting gun fired, I swear it felt like the bow of the canoe beneath me actually raised up out of the water as Bob began to churn, and we lapped our competitor, who, by the way, never challenged me to a canoe race again.

At that time, Bob was director of habitat resources in the old resource protection division of Parks and Wildlife, a unit that was set up to aggressively defend the natural resources of Texas, including our rivers and streams, against all manner of threats—pipelines, reservoirs, highways, and more. On the side, Bob Spain was (and still is) one of the foremost canoe racers in America. He has competed at the highest levels of the sport, and along with his life partner, Joy Emhoff, is among the most well-known paddlers in the nation.

But more than a champion contender, Bob is a champion of the sport itself and here on these pages the reader will find literally everything you need to know about paddling, its equipment and protocols, and its techniques. There is no person more qualified to present this information and Bob Spain does it here in a manner that makes this guide one of the most important titles in the River Books series, a partnership of The Meadows Center for Water and the Environment and Texas A&M University Press. It is hard to imagine that anyone is more dedicated to safe and responsible participation in this awesome outdoor sport than Bob Spain and it is an absolute honor for us to publish this seminal work.

Just as significantly, Spain introduces us to one of the most important outdoor recreation resources, our growing system of Texas Paddling Trails, largely originated by Bob and our colleague Melissa Parker. In a state with such a paucity of publicly available outdoor recreation opportunities, access to our rivers and streams is a godsend for outdoor enthusiasts of all ages. There was a time when significant opposition to public use of Texas waterways existed as riparian landowners (in many cases justifiably) saw the potential impacts this might have on their riverside lands. Today, communities across our state have come to understand that well developed and organized paddling trails bring significant economic benefit to rural Texas and, as a result, we now have one of the most extensive series of official paddling trails in the country. In this book, Bob will introduce you to some of his favorites.

Texas's population will double in the next fifty years yet we permit more water to be withdrawn from many of our natural streams than is actually in them. As Bob would attest, those who increasingly use our rivers and streams often come to love and even defend them from the many threats that these waterways face. The author concludes with inspiring tales of the challenges everyday conservation heroes confront to protect our rivers, lakes, and coasts. We owe a debt of gratitude to these river champions and to Bob Spain who so thoroughly and eloquently advocate for preserving these vital natural resources. And thanks to our partner Recreational Equipment, Inc. (REI), who helped make this book possible.

So enjoy every page and get out on the water, but more importantly, help take responsibility for conserving local waterways so the joys of paddling will be there for our children.

*—Andrew Sansom*

Executive Director, The Meadows Center for Water
and the Environment at Texas State University

# Preface

I remember the first time I went paddling. It was not in a canoe, but a small, aluminum, flat-bottom boat. What I remember most is how difficult it was to paddle. The boat was wide, and when I sat in the middle, I could hardly reach the water. The paddle I used was actually an oar, which was heavy and cumbersome. I'm glad I didn't let this experience sour me from trying again in a recreational canoe. You know, one of those colorful crafts you see at canoe liveries. Again, the experience was not that enjoyable as I still had received no instruction, and I unsuccessfully wove my way across the lake. I still learned a few things by "trial and error," and I knew I wanted to learn more.

The purpose of this book is to introduce you to "canoeing," my favorite sport and pastime, and to acquaint you with the Texas Parks and Wildlife Department's State Paddling Trails Program. Several chapters give a brief history of canoeing and some basic information on types of canoes, equipment, safety, and the correct way to paddle. I hope that everyone who wants to learn will embrace and enjoy the sport that has provided many hours of recreation, exercise, and adventure for me over the past thirty years.

If you are new to the sport, I have provided tips that should get you started in the right direction and help you avoid the pitfalls that frustrate novice paddlers. If you want to improve your paddling technique, I have provided some basic instruction that should help you hone your skills. Even if you are an experienced paddler, the descriptions of my favorite paddling trails should entice you to get out and enjoy Texas' waterways.

# Acknowledgments

I could not have completed the book without the encouragement and support of my wife, Joy. She not only paddled the stern of our canoe, while we surveyed the paddling trails, but she also created original artwork, figures, photos, and read and critiqued the manuscript for content. Without her, I could not have completed this book. A number of the maps, figures, and tables were also created by my stepson, Joshua Bailey, a cartographer. My Austin neighbors, Brad and Colleen Belk, paddled a number of the trails with Joy and me and helped with transportation and shuttles. Brad also mapped a number of our field trips with his GPS receiver. My friends and colleagues at Texas Parks and Wildlife Department provided data, maps, photos, and advice on the book's content. In particular, thanks to Melissa Parker, Ron Smith, and Shelly Plante for their time and input, and also for managing the state's Paddling Trails Program. Chase Fountain provided a number of images of wildlife and river scenes. Cindy Loeffler provided advice and information of the state's water planning process. Thanks also to Jerry Rashall, Tim Bister, Vanessa Nease, Bob Sweeney, Rufus Stephens, Matt Nelson, and Charles Hubbard with Texas Parks and Wildlife Department for their advice and information. Mike Dussere provided information concerning the Water Oriented Recreation District. My friend and expert canoeist, Peter Heed, reviewed sections on canoes, paddling equipment, and paddling instruction. I am indebted to a number of trail sponsors and park managers, for without them, the State Paddling Trails Program would not exit. In particular, Mark Kramer, stewardship coordinator for Armand Bayou Nature Center, provided expertise and reviewed the section on the Armand Bayou Paddling Trail. Matt Shelley, South Llano State Park superintendent, provided comments concerning the manuscript.

Thanks to Jeremy Ward, the curator of the Canadian Canoe Museum, for providing a tour of the museum and images for the book. Dianne Wassenich, program manager of the San Marcos River Foundation, provided valuable information about the foundation and the San Marcos River. Thanks to Shannon Davies, Stacy Eisenstark, and all the folks at Texas A&M University Press for their expertise and efforts in making this book a reality. The generous financial support of Recreational Equipment Incorporated made this publication possible. Thanks also to REI for their Outdoor School that promotes canoeing and other outdoor sports. Thanks to Dr. Jim Kimmel who developed the idea of preparing a book on paddling trails and the opportunity to write it. Certainly, it would not be possible to name everyone who has provided some assistance and encouragement, to all those not named above, thanks. Last but not least, thanks to the Meadows Center for Water and the Environment, and my dear friend, Andy Sansom, for his efforts to conserve Texas' Natural Resources and support of the River Book Series.

# Bob Spain's Canoeing Guide and Favorite Texas Paddling Trails

# 1 Getting Started

After thirty years of paddling, I sometimes forget how much I have learned until I see a new paddler enter the water and immediately crash into the bank or zigzag down the river in a canoe that is totally out of control.

If you are a newcomer, a few basic tips will make your paddling experience much more enjoyable. Seeking advice from someone who is experienced and following their guidance will make all the difference. I was fortunate to have several seasoned paddlers kind enough to show me the basic strokes early in my paddling career. Since then, I have worked diligently to improve my technique, and over the past twenty years or so, I have taught others to paddle. Although I've been canoeing for many years, I still seek advice to improve and perfect my skills.

Local canoe clubs are helpful, and some even organize outings and provide boats that newcomers can try. You can also rent a boat from a canoe livery. Liveries have a variety of canoes and kayaks for rent and some even let you paddle different models to see what you like, which is important for your paddling experience. Choosing a basic recreational canoe for your first experience is advisable because they are stable, maneuverable, and forgiving when you make a mistake (fig. 1.1). Most rental canoes are tandem boats that are designed for two paddlers. These range in length from about 14 to 17 feet. While some canoes are designed for a single paddler, most people choose to paddle with a partner. If a friend has canoed before, take him or her along to help guide the canoe and give you advice along the way. Also seek advice from the people at the canoe livery. They should be able to recommend a canoe.

Canoes come in all shapes and sizes, from long, lightweight, touring, and racing canoes, to shorter, heavier recreational ones that are more maneuverable. Choosing the right canoe is determined by the type of paddling you are interested in. When I am asked, "Which canoe would you recommend?" my short answer is, "That depends upon the type of boating you want to do." Do you want to paddle on rivers, lakes, or streams? Or do you want to take short outings

**FIGURE 1.1.** Recreational canoe.
Photo Courtesy of Johnson Outdoors

or take longer trips and camp overnight? Would you like to try your hand at whitewater or are you content to float down a quiet meandering stream that is peaceful and serene? Would you prefer a slow, stable, and easy-to-handle canoe, or one that is fast, tippy, and tends to go in a straight line? There is a boat for everyone and many brands for every kind of paddling experience.

After choosing a suitable canoe, you will need to learn a few basic paddle strokes to make your paddling experience successful. Oh sure, you can jump in a canoe and try your luck without any instruction, but I assure you that a little instruction will help you avoid the frustration of helplessly zigzagging or running your canoe into banks.

There are several ways to learn the basics of canoeing in addition to this book. Local canoe clubs sometimes provide instruction to help newcomers get started, and some canoe liveries have instructors who give basic lessons. The American Canoe Association (www.americancanoe.org) and the United States Canoe Association (www.uscanoe.org) have trained teachers who offer basic instruction. There are also videos for purchase that illustrate the different types of canoes and how to paddle.

# 2 A Brief History of Canoes and Their Origin in North America

Native Americans in North America used canoes for transportation and carrying game or other commodities. While basic canoe designs were similar among tribes, the materials used in construction differed significantly. Canoes from different regions were made of natural building materials found locally. Some were made from plant materials (trees, bark, and tree roots) while others were made of animal by-products (skins and bones).

## Dugout Canoes

The origin of the word "canoe" comes from the Carib word "kenu," which means "dugout." These crafts were used by the Carib Indians of the Caribbean Islands to travel from island to island. When Christopher Columbus first saw these craft, he said:

> They are not so wide because they are made of a single log of timber, but a galley could not keep up with them in rowing for their motion is a thing beyond belief.[1]

A dugout canoe may sound crude to the uninformed observer. But, when fashioned by a master boatbuilder from the northwest coast of North America, it's a thing of beauty. Known for their colorful canoes, native craftsmen colored their boats with designs of fish, eagles, and other wildlife (fig. 2.1). Since large redwood trees were available in the area, some of the larger canoes made by the Native Americans were 40 to 60 feet long with high sides. They were used by a number of tribes, particularly the Haida, Nootka, Kwakiutl, and Bella Coola, in the rough coastal water for travel and for hunting whales.

## Birch Bark Canoe

No discussion of North American canoes would be complete without a discussion of the "bark" canoe. Bark canoes were built by native tribes like the Algonquin, Cree, and Ojibwa who occupied the deciduous forests of what is now southern Canada and the northern part of the present-day United States.[2] The outer sur-

**FIGURE 2.1.** Dugout, made by Pacific Northwest Native Americans.
Courtesy of Michael Cullen / Canadian Canoe Museum

**FIGURE 2.2.** Birch bark canoe.
Courtesy of Michael Cullen / Canadian Canoe Museum

face of the canoe was covered by tree bark with an internal frame made of tree branches or small tree saplings. Straight tree branches or possibly tree saplings were stripped of bark and then fashioned into gunwales and bent to form the canoe's ribs. While different types of bark were used in different regions, birch bark was favored in areas where the trees were plentiful (fig. 2.2). Why birch bark? It was easy to harvest, durable, pliable, lightweight, and waterproof. Birch bark canoes, often depicted in westerns, had rounded, turned-up ends, white and black colored bark on the sides with black tree pitch that sealed the seams, and rawhide lacing or spruce roots that held the bark to a wood frame.

## Skin Canoes and Kayaks

Tribes living in the extreme northern part of the continent, where trees were scarce or nonexistent, had to rely on other materials to fashion boats. Instead of canoes, kayaks were the primary means of transportation.[3] To deal with the freezing temperatures, kayaks offered several advantages. Using sealskins to cover a frame made of driftwood or animal bones, the Inuit people created a craft that was light and had a deck to keep out cold water (fig. 2.3). The decking that covered the top of the kayak made a watertight craft, and if the boat capsized, the paddler could perform a kayak roll (sometimes referred to as an "Eskimo roll") to right the boat. These sleek kayaks were built for speed and used to pursue swimming game: caribou, polar bears, and seals. A second type of boat, called an "umiak" was open on the top and resembled a canoe. Also covered with animal skins, umiaks were used for hunting larger animals like the bearded or bladdernose seals, beluga whales, narwhals, and even some larger whales.

## Canoe Exploration in North America

Since rivers and streams provided pathways for travel in heavily forested regions of North America, the canoe made exploration possible and facilitated European colonization of remote areas of North America. Canoes were essential for trans-

**FIGURE 2.3.** Greenland kayak made in the similar wood and skin construction used by the Inuit. Courtesy of Michael Cullen / Canadian Canoe Museum

porting goods and commodities to trading posts and smaller settlements that sprang up as settlers moved north and west across the continent.

When Captain Meriwether Lewis and Lieutenant William Clark began their expedition in 1804 to explore the western portion of what is now the United States, they learned from the Nez Percé Indians how to create dugout canoes from large pine trees.[4]

## The Canoe and the History of Fur Trade in North America

More than any other factor, the fur trade influenced the exploration, development, and colonization of the western and northern parts of North America. Early history of the fur trade dates back to the 1600s, when the French laid claim to the Saint Lawrence River and adjoining waters. This gave the French access to a network of streams and lakes that were teeming with the beaver that were in high demand in European markets. Beaver and other fur pelts were transported from the interior in large birch bark canoes, through the Great Lakes, down the Saint Lawrence River, and then loaded on ships bound for Europe.

## Voyageurs and Voyagers

Canoes were the mode of transportation for hunters and trappers and were instrumental in the furtherance of the fur trade. As fur trading companies were formed to transport furs in birch bark canoes to the Atlantic coast, a new breed of adventurers was born. In order to transport pelts from the interior to coastal waters, Native Americans and Frenchmen paddled canoes over hundreds of miles, through all kinds of weather and water conditions, to outposts.[5] These paddlers were called "voyageurs," which means "traveler" in French. Canoes that were used to transport furs from the inland waters to rendezvous sites on the Great Lakes were roughly 24 to 28 feet long and carried four to six voyageurs.

Voyageurs would then load the furs onto larger voyager canoes bound for the Atlantic coast. These larger vessels were about 32 to 40 feet long and held eight to ten voyageurs. As the demand for furs grew, the flourishing fur trade gave rise to canoe building centers that produced larger birch bark freighter canoes.[6]

One account lists a large voyager canoe that was 36 feet long and 6 feet wide.[7] This large-volume canoe could carry 3 tons of furs and other supplies and eight or ten paddlers (fig. 2.4).

The artist's illustration is of a voyager canoe that was used to transport trade goods and supplies from European sailing ships to rendezvous. These enormous canoes were 36 feet long, 6 feet wide and could carry 3 tons of cargo and voyageurs. A typical cargo list might be:

## Hudson's Bay Company

While the French were first to establish a successful fur trading network with the indigenous people, the British also were a major player in the fur trade. In the late 1600s a corporation was formed that had a profound influence upon the fur trade in the lands that drain into Hudson Bay. Originally called "the Honourable Company of Adventures," the Hudson's Bay Company developed a fur trading monopoly in the area, which later became the north-central United States and the vast majority of lands that later became Canada. Established as a corporation in 1670, the Hudson's Bay Company (HBC) developed a network of outposts that stretched across 1.5 million acres that drained into Hudson Bay. In fact, they were the largest land owner in North America.[1]

While the French traders traveled into the interior to meet and trade with the Native Americans, the British Hudson's Bay Company relied on local tribes to paddle their birch bark canoes to HBC outposts on the shores of Hudson Bay.[2] In exchange for the furs, the HBC traded iron implements, knives, blankets, woven cloth, and other commodities to the native inhabitants. Because the dense forested areas made overland travel difficult, the only way to transport goods was by birch bark canoes. Fur pelts that arrived at the outposts were loaded on sailing ships bound for European markets. Like no other, the Hudson's Bay Company developed a fur trading monopoly with Native Americans who lived in the area.

The company's head was Sir George Simpson, who also served as the unofficial governor for the western portion of Canada. Since the company was the only de facto government in the area, they controlled the fur trade; the business flourished for a century without major competition.[3]

Today, the company is still in operation with ninety retail stores in Canada. As the oldest corporation in North America, Hudson's Bay Company has numerous holdings in the United States, including Lord and Taylor, Saks Fifth Avenue, and Neiman Marcus (Hudson's Bay Company, www.hbc.com).

---

1. J. Jennings, "The Canoe Frontier," in *The Canoe, a Living Tradition* (Toronto: Firefly Books, 2002), 38, 39.
2. Ibid.
3. Ibid.

**FIGURE 2.4.** Large voyager canoe carrying furs and cargo

Trade goods: 4,000 to 5,000 lbs. of trade goods (iron implements, knives, blankets, woven cloth, firearms, pots, and other commodities)

Food: hard biscuits, rum, salt pork, beans, flour, sugar, and tobacco

Supplies: cooking utensils, kettles, pots, tents, tarps, medical supplies, carrying packs, guns and ammunition, extra paddles, steering oars, poles, extra birch bark, pine tar, other valuables, and money

Over the years the reputation of the voyageurs grew with the fur trade. They were known far and wide for their stamina and marathon paddling trips across the continent. One account of the voyageurs' lifestyle depicted their days as twenty hours of nonstop paddling, broken only by portages with two 90-pound packs.[8] Unfortunately, they were also known for their rowdy behavior and were often disdained by local settlers due to their disrespect for authority and their violent behavior.

The decline in the demand for furs in Europe and the advent of the steam engine and railroad made canoes less essential. Canoes were still the favored means of transportation in remote forested areas of North America, but steam-driven ships could travel faster up or downstream and carry a larger cargo capacity.

## Grand Portage

Then, in 1784 a new fur trading entity, the North West Company, was formed. The investors, a group of Scottish businessmen, recognized an opportunity and established their headquarters at Grand Portage on the banks of Lake Superior. The Grand Portage (fig. 2.5) was a 9-mile overland passage that linked the Pigeon River with Lake Superior. The overland portage was used to avoid the large waterfalls and fast-moving water on the Pigeon River that capsized canoes and claimed the lives of many fur traders over the years. With this strategic location, the company had access to a vast inland river network and clear passage through the Great Lakes and the adjoining rivers to the Atlantic Ocean.

Each summer the North West Company held a rendezvous at Grand Portage, a meeting place where the wintering "north men," who spent their winters trading for furs in the interior, paddled their canoes.[1] Here they met with the "Montreal men" who carried blankets, woven cloth, iron implements, firearms, and other commodities that arrived on sailing ships from Europe. At the North West Company's headquarters, the furs were traded for the supplies and commodities.

Today the Grand Portage is a National Historic Monument that is maintained by the National Park Service. The site is located in extreme northeast Minnesota just north of the town of Grand Marais. The 9-mile portage is a park where hikers and backpackers can follow in the footsteps of fur traders who carried their massive birch bark canoes and furs to the outpost.

I toured the site in the summer of 2014. A restoration included replicas of the Great Hall, Warehouse, and other buildings. Reenactors at the site, dressed in authentic clothing, depicted the lifestyle that existed during the heyday of the fur trade. There were also replicas of the birch bark canoes on display. One massive birch bark canoe, more than 40 feet long, rested near the palisade walls (fig. 2.6). Each year a celebration is held at the park to commemorate the rendezvous.

---

1. Beth Drost, "Grand Portage: The Great Carrying Place," National Parks Service, 2014, 14–15.

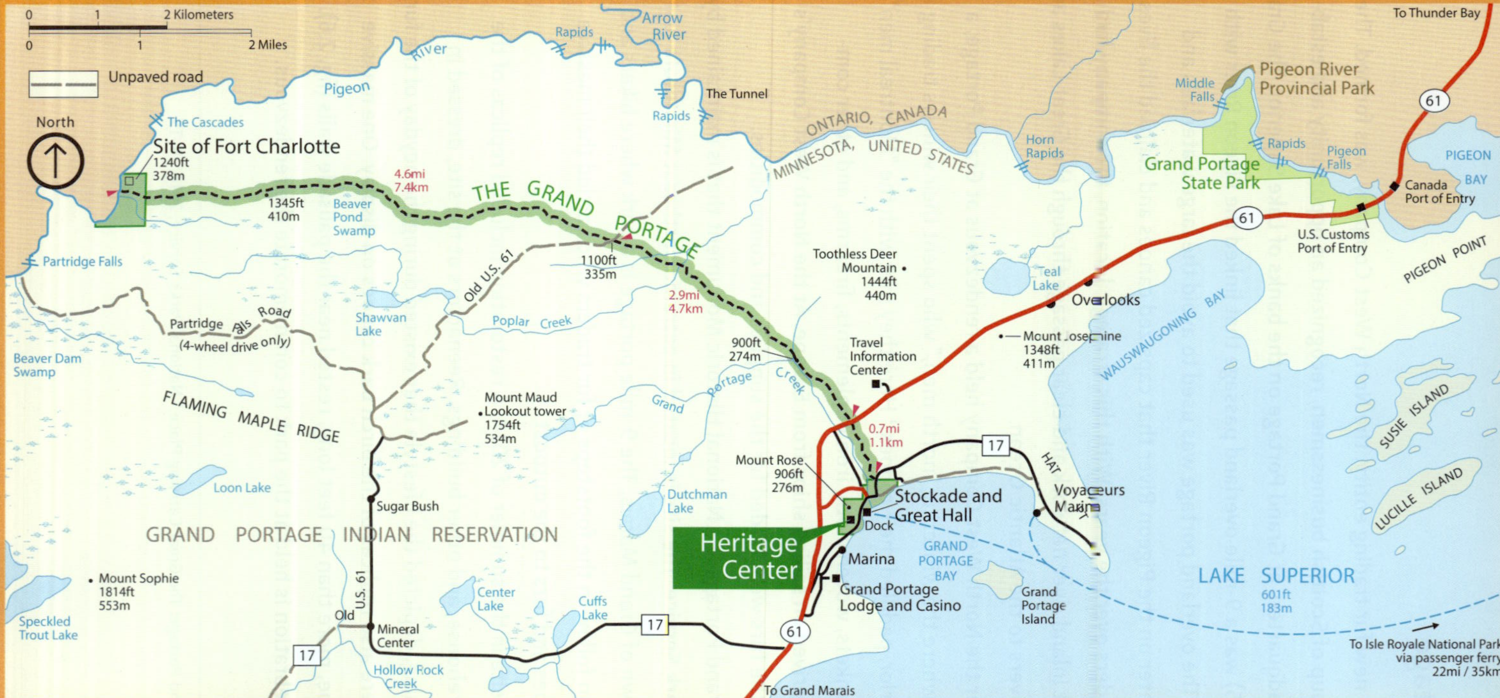


**FIGURE 2.5.** Map of Grand Portage.

Courtesy of National Parks Service

**FIGURE 2.6.** 40-foot canoe at Grand Portage historical site

## The Modern Canoe

The mass producers of canoes that sprung up to support the fur trade shifted gears and began producing a new kind of canoe, one that was not for "work" but for "pleasure." While birch bark canoes had always been the standard, their popularity waned when the supply of large trees ran out.

During the early 1800s, Canadians began to build dugout canoes that were fashioned after the design of the Native Americans.[9] These canoes, with basswood hulls, were shaped with axes, planes, and drawknives, which enabled builders to create wooden canoes that had rounded sides, pointed ends, and were only three quarters of an inch thick. European immigrants experimented with new techniques that were less labor intensive. They began building canoes out of wood strips, boards, planks, and battens fastened together around a frame and waterproofed. This facilitated the mass production of canoes.

From the 1880s to the mid-1900s, the Canadian canoe industry grew. Peterborough and nearby Lakefield, Ontario, became the manufacturing centers of wooden canoes.[10] Today, Peterborough is known for its canoe history and is the home of the Canadian Canoe Museum, housing more than six hundred canoes and kayaks.

Meanwhile, in Maine, canoe builders also used a ridged wooden frame, but covered it with canvas and applied a waterproof coating. This technique eliminated the time-consuming task of sealing the many seams in a wooden canoe.

While there were a number of canoe designers and builders who contributed to the development of recreational canoes, one of the more noted was J. H. Rushton from Canton, New York. In 1873 Rushton made his first canoe, and over the next thirty years he designed and manufactured many lightweight recreational canoes. One of his most popular canoes was the "Indian Girl." This canoe was lightweight, maneuverable, and sleek in design. Over the years, Rushton was known for building many lightweight canoes, and in 1879, he built an ultralight 10-foot canoe that weighed only seventeen and a half pounds. The boat was built for George Washington Sears, a shoemaker turned wanderer. The canoe was called the *Nessmuk*, and over the next few years, Mr. Sears traveled hundreds of miles in his lightweight canoe.

During the first half of the 1900s, canoe builders continued to refine their methods of building wood and canvas canoes that were lighter, more colorful, and more streamlined. During the mid-twentieth century, the development of even lighter, stronger materials, like aluminum and fiberglass, created more competition.

Today there is a cornucopia of canoes for paddlers to choose. There are plastic recreational play boats, kayaks that are pedal driven, sea kayaks, Olympic design canoes and kayaks, downriver canoes, whitewater canoes, stand-up paddleboards, and many other types to choose from (fig. 2.7).

**FIGURE 2.7.** Examples of different kinds of boats.
Courtesy of Sandy Yonley

# 3 Canoes, Their Design, and Other Paddle Crafts

## Wood/Canvas Canoes

Although several canoe companies began to build wood/canvas canoes, the most prominent company started in Old Town, Maine, around 1895. Originally called the Indian Old Town Canoe Company, it was incorporated in 1903 as the Old Town Canoe Company and would become one of the largest canoe and kayak manufacturing companies in the world. Their beautiful wood/canvas canoes adorned with brass screws and brass trim are commercially available today and are a far cry from early dugouts or bark canoes (fig. 3.1). New wood/canvas canoes start at around $2,800 and go up in cost from there.

**FIGURE 3.1.** (*Above; and facing page*) Canvas over wood canoe.
Courtesy of Ralph Scarpino

## Wood Canoes

Canoes made of wood are still the choice of some paddlers because nothing can compare to the beautiful wood grain and sleek finish. Wood is also a popular choice for those who want to create their own canoe. Built as family projects, constructed in the garage or workshop, these canoes are functional but their design is often crude. Sometimes built from scratch or from a kit, wood canoes are often made of plywood or wood strips, and when covered with a layer of fiberglass and resin for waterproofing, become a seaworthy vessel. Canoes made of spruce, cedar, mahogany, or cherry wood are works of art. Modern commercially made wooden canoes look more like fine furniture than the early wooden ones.

Best suited for paddling on lakes or deep water, wooden canoes are fragile and when punctured are difficult to repair. The canoe's wood exterior requires many hours of handwork and is very labor intensive to build. Designs that are more elaborate can cost $7,000 or more (fig. 3.2).

## Fiberglass Canoes

In 1932 a researcher for Owens-Illinois Glass Company, Dale Kleist,[1] passed a jet of compressed air over a stream of molten glass and produced fibers. The resulting wool-like material was patented by Owens Corning in 1936. When "fiberglass" material was combined with an epoxy resin, the process created a

**FIGURE 3.2.** Wood strip C-1 canoe

composite material that was lightweight, inherently strong, and waterproof. It was initially used for home insulation, but fiberglass has many other uses, such as car bodies and parts, domes, and other architectural features.

Individuals began to experiment with the material to make boat hulls. While there is some question as to who first began to mass-produce fiberglass canoes, Old Town Canoe Company introduced a Rushton model in 1960 that weighed only ten and a half pounds.[2]

The popularity of fiberglass canoes grew rapidly. They are lighter and cheaper than wood and wood/canvas canoes, are waterproof, and can be easily repaired.

The production of a fiberglass canoe begins with a rigid mold. Next, a thin resin gel coat is applied to the inner surface of the mold. This gives the canoe color and protects the exterior of the canoe. A layer of fiberglass cloth is placed inside the mold, and epoxy resin is then poured in the mold. Once the epoxy saturates the cloth, the excess is removed and the cloth is allowed to set. The resulting stiff hull is removed from the mold and reinforced with ribs and thwarts, seats are added, and a canoe is formed. These canoes are less expensive than wood and wood/canvas. Fiberglass canoes range in price from approximately $1,000 to $2,500 (fig. 3.3).

## Aluminum Canoes

Another popular material for the manufacture of recreational canoes is aluminum. While aluminum and aluminum alloys had already been used to manufacture airplane bodies, the use of aluminum in the manufacture of canoes did not occur until the 1940s.

In 1944, during a trip in the Adirondacks, William Huffman grew weary of portaging his heavy wood/canvas canoe. Huffman was an executive for the Northrup Grumman Corporation, a company that had manufactured aluminum airplanes for several years to support the war effort. After returning from his canoe trip, Mr. Huffman convinced two company heads, Leroy Grumman and Jake Swirbul, to build a prototype aluminum canoe.[3] The timing was perfect since

**FIGURE 3.3.** Fiberglass canoe

the war effort was winding down and the company was looking for new products to enable it to continue its business. One company advertisement boasted a 13-foot, 38-pound canoe that "even a woman can carry."[4]

Aluminum canoes were well received by the paddling public because these lighter-weight canoes were easier to transport, portage around obstructions in rivers, and never needed to be resurfaced.

Another company that pioneered the manufacture of aluminum canoes in America was Alumacraft Canoes. While there were other companies that produced aluminum canoes, these two were the leaders. Both companies changed ownership over the years, but they continue to make aluminum canoes today, although the larger part of their market is manufacturing motorized fishing boats.

One negative aspect of aluminum canoes is that they are noisy when you hit a rock or other obstacle in the water, and the resulting battle scars are impossible to reshape or remove. I bought my first aluminum canoe in the 1980s and still have it. It shows some dents and scratches but continues to be a great, lightweight, recreational canoe.

Aluminum canoes are also the choice of paddlers who choose to race recreational canoes. Over the years, the Alumacraft lightweight voyager canoe has become the favorite of many racers in Texas. An Alumacraft canoe has won the Buffalo Bayou Regatta, the Texas Canoe and Kayak Racing Association State Aluminum Championships, and the United States Canoe Association Stock Aluminum National Championships, to name a few. Aluminum canoes start at about $1,000 (fig. 3.4).

## Polyethylene Canoes

Because polyethylene does not absorb water, is relatively light yet tough and flexible, its uses are widespread for the manufacture of many types of products. Today, a person can hardly walk through their kitchen or bathroom without seeing items made of polyethylene.

Polyethylene kayaks first appeared on the scene for whitewater paddling in the 1970s. The material's high-impact resistance made it a perfect fit. Due to the low production cost of plastic kayaks and canoes, more crafts are made from this material than other higher-priced materials. While the majority of the recreational market is for polyethylene kayaks, low cost polyethylene canoes are also a popular choice for first-time buyers, novice paddlers, and those who only paddle occasionally.

The production of polyethylene canoes begins with a heated mold that is filled with plastic pellets. The heated mold liquefies the pellets, and once the plastic dries, a hull is formed. Some polyethylene canoes have internal aluminum frames, while others may have seats suspended from the gunwales that serve as thwarts. Polyethylene canoes are very inexpensive, but they do have several negative aspects. The material is heavier than aluminum or composites, and it can flex or "oil can" when paddled. Hot sunshine can also cause the material to lose its shape when left outside. If punctured, the material is difficult to repair. The cost of polyethylene canoes starts at $300 to $400 (fig. 3.5).

**FIGURE 3.4.** Alumacraft aluminum canoe.
Courtesy of Barry Tse

**FIGURE 3.5.** Polyethylene canoe.
Courtesy of Johnson Outdoors

## Kevlar Canoes

In 1965 DuPont developed a new lightweight material called Kevlar that has had a profound impact upon canoe and kayak construction. When mixed with resin, Kevlar creates a composite material that is lighter and stronger than fiberglass. The material is well known for its use in body armor (bulletproof vests). Many lightweight racing and touring canoes are made of Kevlar.

The construction of Kevlar canoes is similar to the process for producing fiberglass canoes. First, sheets of Kevlar are placed in a mold and epoxy resin is added. To strengthen the hull, foam is laid inside the hull covering the bottom and strips of foam are laid inside the hull along the sides to serve as ribs. Next, a second sheet of Kevlar can be laid over the foam and more resin added. Excess resin is then removed from the hull with a vacuum pump, creating a lighter-weight, finished product. Once the hull is removed from the mold, gunwales are added to stiffen the hull, seats are installed, and a canoe is formed.

Kevlar is very difficult to puncture; however, a sharp object in the water can cut the fibers. When this occurs, repairing poses a problem. When a Kevlar patch is sanded, the resulting finish is fuzzy. To solve this, many boat shops make repairs with fiberglass. Kevlar canoes start at about $2,000 (fig. 3.6).

**FIGURE 3.6.** Kevlar canoe

## Royalex Canoes

Royalex was a product developed in 1970 by the Uniroyal Company and became very popular for the construction of recreational canoes. Because this material has been such an integral part of the canoe and kayak industry, I feel obligated to mention it. However, Royalex is no longer available. Regrettably, PolyCorp, the sole manufacturer of Royalex, shut down its facility in December 2013, and the production of Royalex canoes ended in 2014.

Canoe liveries favored Royalex canoes because they were rugged and lasted for years. Royalex was made of several laminated layers and a layer of foam. These canoes were sometimes called ABS canoes because their official name, acrylonitrile butadiene styrene, was difficult to pronounce.

ABS canoes survive rocky streams and are, therefore, favored by many recreational canoeists and whitewater paddlers. Only time will tell if another material will take its place.

## Carbon Fiber Canoe

The history of carbon fiber dates back to 1956 when Union Carbide opened its Parma Technical Center near Cleveland, Ohio.[5] Two years later a research physicist, Dr. Roger Bacon, who worked at the plant, made an important discovery while working with graphite. When he heated graphite under pressure, it formed

**FIGURE 3.7.** Carbon fiber canoe.
Courtesy of Savage River

carbon fibers that were stronger and stiffer than any material of the same weight. One year later two researchers at the same plant patented a process that produced carbon fibers and carbon cloth. This material, like fiberglass and Kevlar, can be mixed with resin to create a lighter and stronger composite material.

During the next few years, the military began to look at the material for various uses. Since its development some fifty plus years ago, carbon fiber has become the favored product for many applications when weight and strength are important. Some uses include aircraft brakes, military and commercial planes, sporting goods, powerboat hulls, and canoes and kayaks.

Most racing canoes and higher-priced recreational canoes are made of carbon fiber. Sometimes used in combination with Kevlar, carbon fiber canoes are lightweight and highly prized by canoe racers and long distance paddlers. A sleek carbon fiber racing canoe can cost $3,500 to $4,500 (fig. 3.7).

## Other Paddle Crafts

In addition to canoes, several other types of paddle craft are popular in Texas and across the nation. Kayaks are one of the more popular paddle crafts for paddlers of all ages. This is particularly true of youth and novice paddlers. In fact, it's my opinion that more solo kayaks are sold to youth and novice paddlers than any other type of paddle craft. Kayaks differ from canoes in several ways. First, kayaks sit lower in the water than canoes, and for that reason, recreational kayaks tend to be more stable. Kayaks also have decks that cover the bow and stern area, with an opening (cockpit) in the center where the paddler sits. A skirt can be installed on the cockpit to keep out the water.

Over the last twenty-five to thirty years another type of kayak has become more and more popular. It is called a "sit-on-top" and differs from other kayaks in several ways. A deck covers the entire surface and there is no cockpit; instead, there is a depression in the deck where the paddler sits. There are also depressions in the deck where a paddler rests his/her feet. This design makes the craft unsinkable. Additionally, the craft is much easier to launch and reenter if you take an unplanned swim (fig. 3.8).

Last but not least, over the past ten years a new type of paddle craft has risen in popularity. In fact, the craft has introduced many new paddlers to the sport of paddling. From its coastal origin, the surfboard has been reborn as a paddle craft. It is called a stand-up paddleboard, or SUP. Just like the surfboard, paddlers stand on the SUP and paddle with a long single-blade paddle (fig. 3.9).

Based upon my observations while on the Lady Bird Lake Paddling Trail in Austin, this craft is popular with teenagers and young adults. To my surprise,

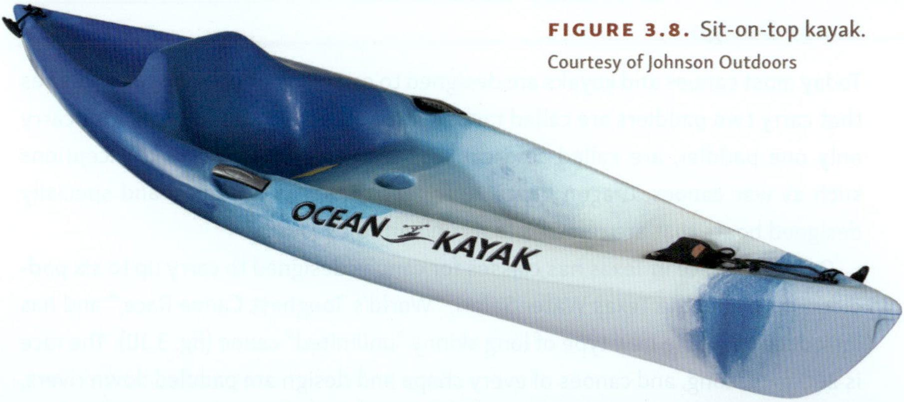


**FIGURE 3.8.** Sit-on-top kayak.
Courtesy of Johnson Outdoors

**FIGURE 3.9.** SUP (stand-up paddleboard).
Courtesy of Savage River

over half of the 450 paddle craft I witnessed, while paddling a 4-mile stretch of the trail on a busy weekend, were SUPs. The remainder were all other vessels, including canoes, kayaks, and rowing boats.

One disadvantage to keep in mind is that a SUP paddler stands on the board, which brings the paddler's center of gravity higher than if he or she were sitting in a canoe. As a result, the board is less stable. SUPs can also be difficult to maneuver on choppy water or in windy conditions.

## Canoe Design

Today most canoes and kayaks are designed to carry one or two paddlers. Canoes that carry two paddlers are called tandem canoes, or C-2s, and canoes that carry only one paddler, are called solo canoes, or C-1s. There are some exceptions such as war canoes, dragon boats, outrigger canoes, inflatables, and specially designed boats that are referred to as unlimited canoes.

One canoe race in Texas has classes for canoes designed to carry up to six paddlers. It's called the Texas Water Safari, "World's Toughest Canoe Race," and has introduced a whole new type of long skinny "unlimited" canoe (fig. 3.10). The race is 260 miles long, and canoes of every shape and design are paddled down rivers, carried across log jams, around dams, and paddled across San Antonio Bay.

As mentioned earlier, there is a canoe for every type of water or paddling experience, and no one canoe is perfect for all conditions. Generally speaking, canoes that are long and narrow are fast and unstable, and those that are shorter and wider are slow and stable. Recreational canoes are more stable, easier to steer, and will carry plenty of extra gear. These canoes will accommodate three adults or two adults and several youths.

The shape of a canoe's hull determines its stability and maneuverability. Canoes that have wide flat bottoms have good initial stability. This means they are stable when you enter the canoe or when you are sitting still. Those that are narrow and have rounded bottoms, have little initial stability (fig. 3.11).

**FIGURE 3.10.** Unlimited canoe.
Courtesy of Texas Water Safari / Ashley Landis

FIGURE 3.11. Hull shape of bottom of canoe

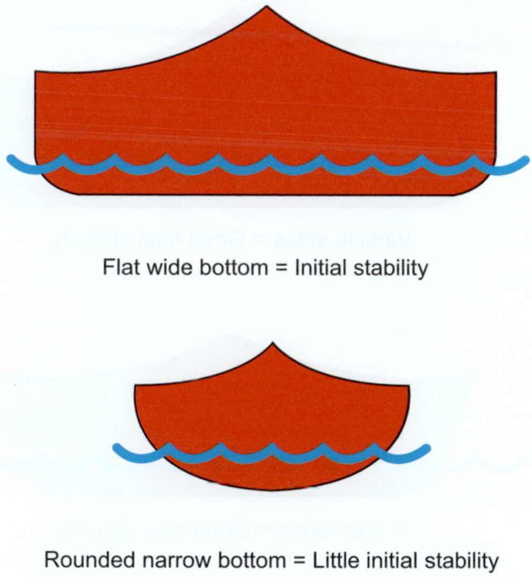


The configuration of the sides of the canoe determines the "final" stability of the canoe. If the sides rise vertically from the water's surface when the canoe is sitting in the water, or if the sides flare outward from the keel-line of the canoe, the canoe will have good final stability. This is important since the sides can prevent an unplanned swim when the canoe is leaned either way. If the canoe is leaned to one side, the sides will push against the water's surface and help to right the canoe. However, canoes that have sides that curve inward toward the keel have "tumblehome." These canoes have less final stability and, consequently, the rounded gunwales will allow the canoe to roll over and capsize when the canoe is leaned too far to either side (fig. 3.12).

A long, stiff "gunwale" runs along the top of the sides of a canoe and gives the boat strength. The name "gunwale" comes from sailing ships that had cannons mounted on the sides. A gun wall was built on top of the sides to reinforce the integrity of the ship's hull against the weight and recoil of the cannons. Over time, the name has changed to "gunwales" or, sometimes, "gunnels." There are also braces, called "thwarts," on canoes that stretch across the top and are attached to the gunwales. The rigid braces support the gunwales and protect the canoe's hull (fig. 3.13).

Canoes that have a keel running along the bottom tend to "track," or travel in a straight line. However, when there is no keel, the canoe tends to slide from side to side and not track well. While a keel is helpful for long distance canoe trips, it can be troublesome when paddling shallow streams with rocks (fig. 3.14). On

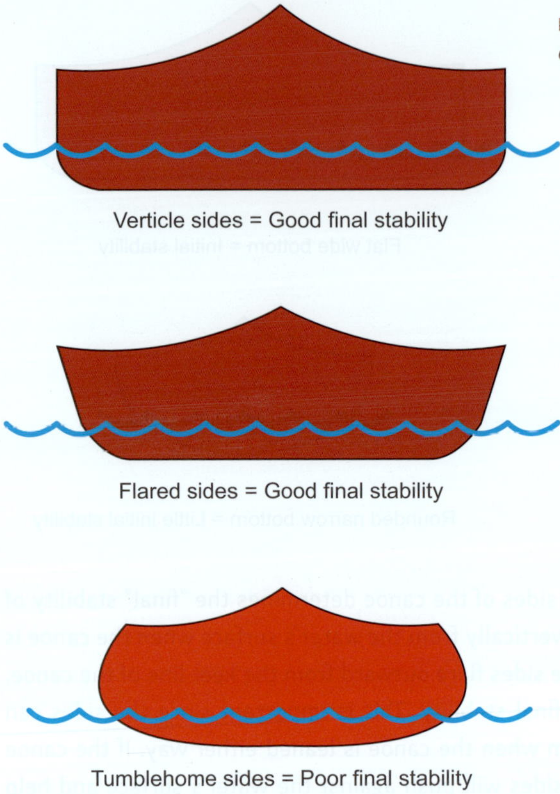


**FIGURE 3.12.** Hull shape of sides of canoe

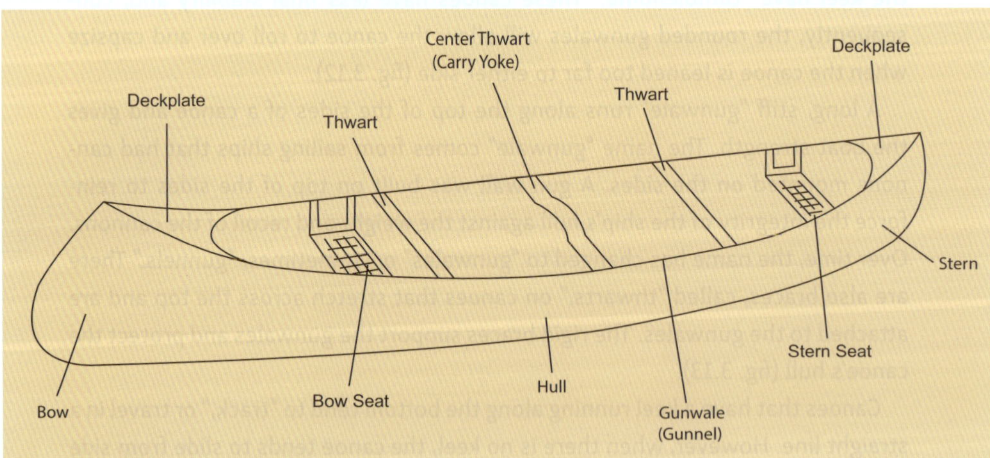


**FIGURE 3.13.** Canoe with parts shown

a recent trip along the South Llano River Paddling Trail, my wife, Joy, and I were paddling our Dagger 17-foot recreational canoe with no keel, while our neighbors (and fellow canoeing enthusiasts), Brad and Colleen Belk, were in an aluminum canoe with a keel. While our canoe skimmed smoothly across the stream's rocky bottom, the keel of the aluminum canoe snagged repeatedly, forcing Brad and Colleen to get in the river on several occasions to keep the boat from hanging up.

Another factor influencing a boat's ability to track in a straight line is the boat's "rocker." Rocker is the amount of upward curve of the bottom of the bow and the stern that is visible when you look at a canoe from the side. To illustrate, if a canoe is sitting on the ground with the center touching the ground, and the bottom of the bow and stern do not touch the ground, the canoe has "rocker." Canoes with "lots of rocker" are easy to turn. This, however, can be counterproductive when the canoe is paddled for a long distance because the canoe will slide from side to side, and a paddler will need to make corrective strokes frequently (fig. 3.15).

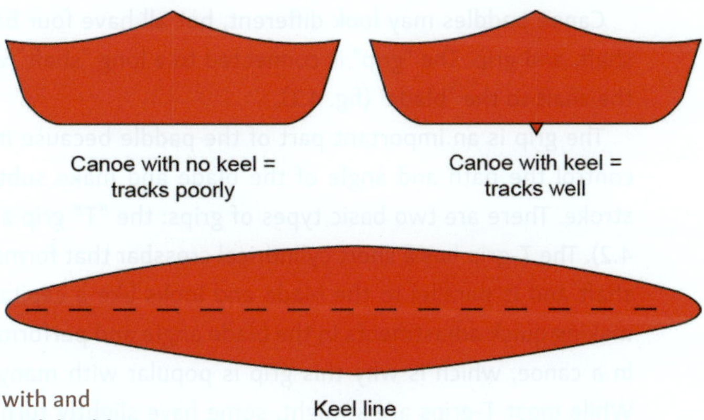


**FIGURE 3.14.** Canoes with and without keel (*top*); canoe with keel-line shown (*bottom*)

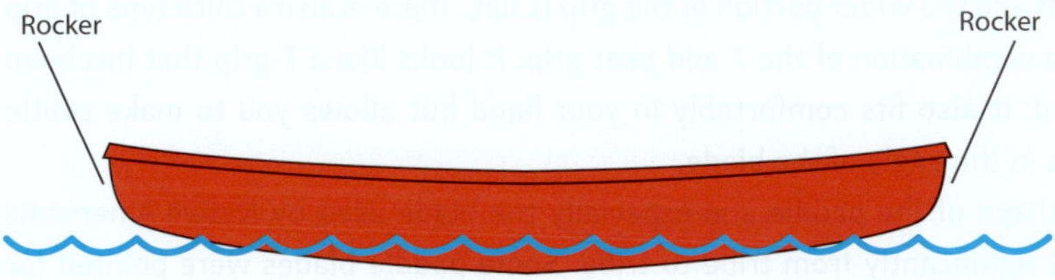


**FIGURE 3.15.** Canoe with rocker

# 4 Paddling Gear

## Canoe Paddles

Canoe paddles, like canoes, come in many shapes and sizes. Some are made of plastic, aluminum, wood, fiberglass, Kevlar, carbon fiber, or a combination of these materials. Inexpensive paddles made of wood or aluminum and plastic start at approximately $35, while the lightweight carbon canoe paddles can cost more than $300.

Canoe paddles may look different, but all have four basic parts: blade, neck, shaft, and grip. The "grip" is connected to a long "shaft" with a "neck" that joins the shaft to the "blade" (fig. 4.1).

The grip is an important part of the paddle because it allows the paddler to control the path and angle of the blade and make subtle changes during the stroke. There are two basic types of grips: the "T" grip and the "pear" grip (fig. 4.2). The *T*-grip has a short cylindrical crossbar that forms a right angle with the shaft and is parallel to the blade and looks like a capital letter *T*. It's ideal for making quick adjustments in the blade angle and performing various maneuvers in a canoe, which is why this grip is popular with many whitewater paddlers. While most *T*-grips are straight, some have slightly turned down ends. *T*-grips are found on many of the less expensive paddles as well.

The second type of grip is the "pear" grip. It is shaped like a flattened pear and fits comfortably in your hand. The smaller part of the "pear" grip is attached to the shaft and the wider portion of the grip is flat. There is also a third type of grip that is a combination of the *T* and pear grip. It looks like a *T*-grip that has been flattened. It also fits comfortably in your hand but allows you to make subtle changes in the angle of the blade.

The shape of the paddle and especially the blade used by Native Americans differed significantly from tribe to tribe. Some paddle blades were pointed for use in battle; others varied in the shape, length, and width. Some were shaped like beaver tails, otter tails, and willow leaves (fig. 4.3). The legendary voyageurs'

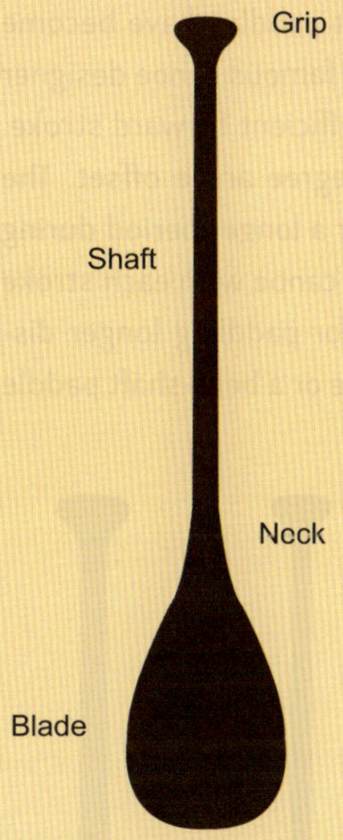


**FIGURE 4.1.** Parts of a canoe paddle

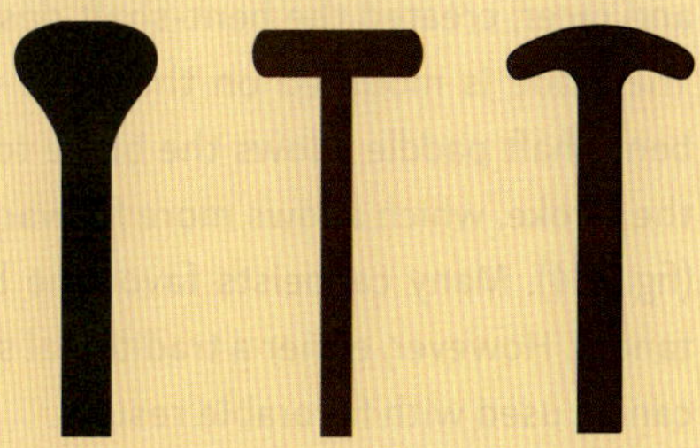

**FIGURE 4.2.** Types of paddle grips

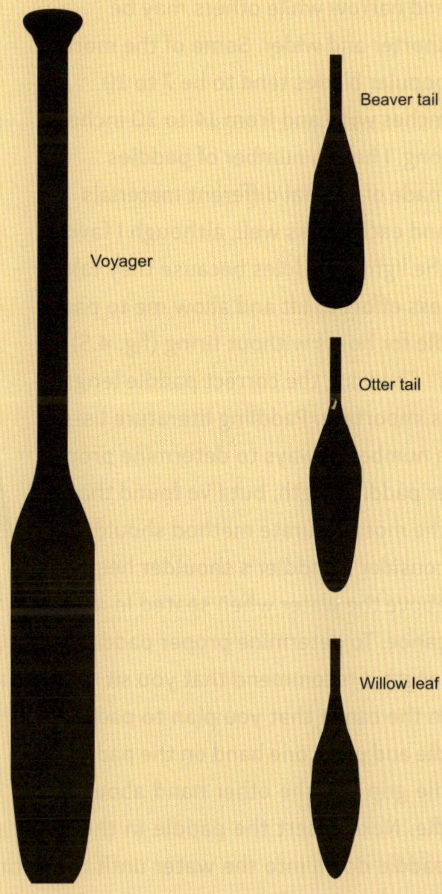


**FIGURE 4.3.** Shapes of early paddle blades

paddles were long and narrow. The narrow blade was easier to pull through the water during the long marathon paddling days.

Traditional canoe paddles are straight, but bent-shaft paddles have become popular over the last thirty to forty years. Gene Jensen, a famous canoe designer and racer, created the bent-shaft design to get a more efficient forward stroke. The blade is mounted on the shaft with a 12- to 14-degree angle offset. The bent-shaft paddle allows the blade to remain vertical for a longer period during the stroke, which allows more forward movement of the canoe with each stroke (fig. 4.4). Many canoeists favor the bent-shaft paddle for paddling longer distances. However, either a traditional straight-shaft paddle or a bent-shaft paddle can be used with favorable results.

Today there are several different blade shapes. Some blades are long and narrow while others may be shorter and wider. Some of the more popular blades tend to be 7 to 10 inches wide and from 14 to 20 inches long. I have a number of paddles made of several different materials and each works well, although I favor the lighter paddles because they take less effort to lift and allow me to paddle for hours without tiring (fig. 4.5).

**FIGURE 4.4.** Bent-shaft paddle

**FIGURE 4.5.** Shapes of modern paddles

Choosing the correct paddle length is important. Paddling literature lists a number of ways to determine proper paddle length, but I've found that the most accurate method should consider a paddler's shoulder height above the water when seated in a canoe. To determine proper paddle length, I recommend that you sit in the canoe that you plan to paddle and place one hand on the paddle grip and the other hand about 6 to 8 inches above to the neck of the paddle. Next, insert the paddle in the water near the side of the canoe. Push the paddle down into the water until the entire blade is submerged. Hold the shaft near the side of your canoe while keeping the shaft perpendicular to the water surface. Next, pull the paddle along the side of the canoe until the paddle blade approaches your hip. If your top hand, which is on the grip, is about eye level, the paddle is about the correct length. If the grip hand is above your head, the paddle is too long. Likewise, if the grip of the paddle is near or below your chin, and/or you have to lean out of the boat to submerge the blade, the paddle is too short. If the paddle is too long or too short, you will not be able to perform an efficient stroke and apply good pressure to the blade.

## Personal Flotation Device (PFD)

It is very important that every person who paddles or rides in a canoe or other watercraft has a US Coast Guard approved personal flotation device (PFD) in the craft. PFDs are also commonly called life jackets because they can save your life. PFDs contain lightweight material that helps you float in water. They are certified by the US Coast Guard and are classified by the amount of flotation they provide. Life jackets are classified as Class I, II, III, IV, or V (table 1). Some PFDs are inflatable and have a $CO_2$ cartridge that fills the jacket when needed. Some inflatable jackets are self-inflating and others have a rip cord that has to be pulled for inflation. Inflatable PFDs are only legal if they are worn, so always read the manufacturer's label for recommended use. Most paddlers choose the Type III PFD because it provides ample flotation and allows plenty of room for arm movement when paddling. I use a Type III PFD.

Every state may have different requirements. For instance, Texas law requires that every person who paddles a canoe, kayak, or other paddle craft must carry a US Coast Guard approved PFD in their boat. It further requires that anyone under thirteen years of age must wear the PFD. Inflatable PFD's are legal, but they must be worn to be legal.

When choosing a PFD, it is important that the PFD fits properly. If it is too tight it can restrict breathing, and if it is too large, it can slip over your head when you fall into the water. There is a simple test to determine if a jacket fits properly. First, put it on, tighten the straps or zipper, then hold up your arms above your head and ask a friend to grasp the shoulder area of the PFD and lift up on it. If it slides up above your face, you need to choose a smaller one or tighten the straps on the jacket.

While state law does not mandate that you wear the PFD, statistics reveal that wearing a PFD can save your life. According to *Saved by the Jacket* (National Safe Boating Council, Inc. 2000), 90 percent of people who drowned were *not* wearing a PFD. The book also chronicles many true-life stories and testimonials of paddlers, fishermen, and other water enthusiasts who were saved from drown-

| Types of Coast Guard Approved PFDs | |
|---|---|
| **Type I PFD**<br>Buoyancy 22 lbs. | Most often used in open, remote or rough water, where rescues could be delayed. Most buoyant, brightly colored, will turn most unconscious wearers face-up. |
| **Type II PFD**<br>Buoyancy 15.5 lbs. | Used for inland, calm water where rescue can occur quickly. Less bulky, often less expensive and many will turn an unconscious person face-up in the water. |
| **Type III PFD**<br>Buoyancy 15.5 lbs. | Used for inland, calm water where rescue can occur quickly. Most comfortable, but most likely will not turn an unconscious person face-up. |
| **Type IV PFD**<br>Buoyancy 16.5–18 lbs. | Cushions, ring buoys and horseshoe buoys. Designed to be thrown to someone and as a backup to a PFD. |
| **Type V PFD**<br>Buoyancy 7.51–22 lbs. | For special uses or conditions as stated on the label. Many must be worn at all times to qualify as an approved PFD. |

ing by wearing their PFDs and lived to tell about it. So, wear your life jacket when you paddle.

## Waterproof Container

Many canoe trips start out as a day of recreation and fun, but that can change quickly by an unplanned swim in the water. If an unexpected swim does occur, contents that are not tied in the canoe may be lost, and items that are not waterproof will be ruined. To protect against this, secure everything in the boat with canoe straps, ropes, or carabiners. Also, take along a waterproof bag or waterproof hard case container for items like food, clothing, cell phones, or cameras. There are lots of waterproof bags to choose from, and some canoe liveries provide bags when you rent a canoe. Some smaller bags are designed with see-through windows for cell phones and GPS receivers. Larger bags are designed to carry sleeping bags, tents, camp stoves, and other gear. Some larger bags even have backpack straps for carrying on portages. All bags have a positive closure at the top, and some have straps to tie the bag in the boat. Makeshift waterproof bags, such as zip-lock bags, are water resistant but not waterproof. Don't soak your change of clothes. And don't end up skipping lunch because your sandwich is soggy because you forgot to use a waterproof bag. If you choose to purchase a bag, prices range from about $10 to more than a $100, depending upon the size of the bag (fig. 4.6).

Waterproof hard cases are also a good choice for protecting delicate items that could get broken in a soft-sided waterproof bag. Hard cases have a waterproof gasket on the lid and latches that seal tightly. The boxes vary in size from smaller ones that will hold a cell phone to large ones that will carry a cook stove and/or sleeping bag (fig. 4.7). Some have a rubber or foam-rubber lining, and you can cut out the foam to fit items more securely. One disadvantage of hard case containers is that they cannot be stuffed into a tight space in the bow or stern and they will have to be lashed to a thwart or under the seat. A list of typical items that should be carried in your canoe on a day trip, or an overnight trip, is shown in appendix 1.

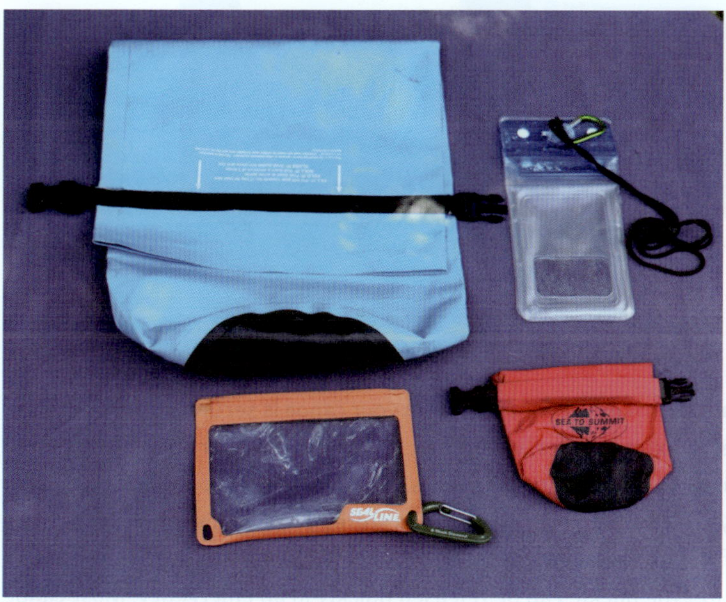


**FIGURE 4.6.** Examples of waterproof bags

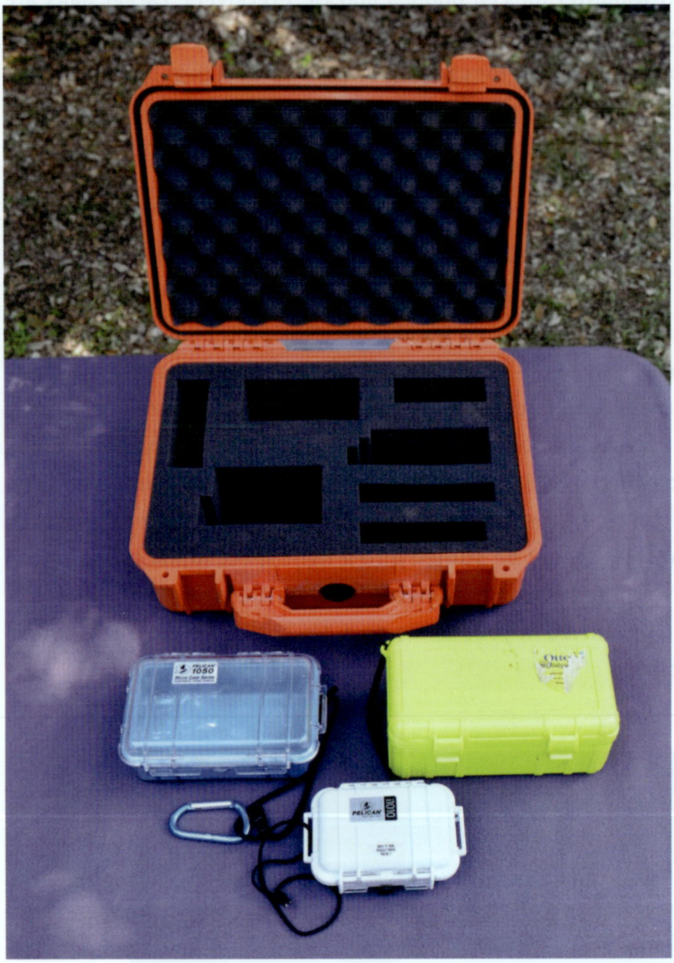

**FIGURE 4.7.** Examples of waterproof cases

## Lanyards

It is important to make sure that all gear in your canoe is secured in case you capsize. Ice chests, extra paddles, water jugs, dry bags, and other equipment should be tied securely to thwarts or canoe seats. A small strand of rope works nicely, or you can buy river straps at sporting goods stores or canoe liveries. River straps are made of webbing and have a spring-loaded buckle that clips to the strap for a secure closure. The buckle can be released quickly in an emergency. Most canoe liveries sell these straps for $10 to $15.

## Painter Lines

Canoes, unlike larger motorized boats, can be launched easily from an earthen bank or small dock. Because some paddling trails have steep banks, the put-in and take-out can be slippery or muddy when wet. A rope or line (painter) attached to the bow and stern of your canoe will make launching and take-outs much easier. The rope is helpful and can be held by one paddler to lower a canoe down to the water or can be used on the bank by a paddler to pull the canoe out of the water. A 6- to 8-foot rope is all that is needed. Although you can attach a longer painter to secure your boat to the bank for temporary docking. If you paddle a solo boat, a painter line is particularly helpful.

## Throw Bags / Rescue Lines

A throw bag is an important item for emergencies. A throw bag is a cloth bag that contains a rope coiled inside with a weight attached (fig. 4.8). If someone capsizes, the throw bag can be tossed to the capsized person so they can be pulled to safety. To perform a rescue, simply hold the end of the rope with one hand and with your other hand throw the bag to the swimmer. If you are in a stream with current, be sure to throw the bag upstream of the swimmer. The current will float the bag back to the swimmer. Once they grasp the line, pull them to safety.

**FIGURE 4.8.** Examples of throw lines / throw bags

# 5 How to Paddle a Canoe

Learning to paddle a canoe is not a difficult task. In fact, many paddlers teach themselves by trial and error. However, to avoid the mistakes and bad habits that can occur along the way, seeking some basic instruction in the beginning will make the experience more successful and enjoyable. Learning to paddle efficiently opens up the outdoors and allows you to paddle longer stretches, extending the adventure of exploring Texas waterways. After a little practice, you can paddle all day long without getting tired, plus you have the added benefit of getting in better shape. Whether you have someone to "show you the ropes" so to speak, or not, I will provide some basic information in the following sections that will get you started in the right direction.

First, there are fundamental tips to keep in mind before you take your first paddle stroke. The resistance of the canoe against the water, its inertia, can be greater than the resistance of the paddle in the water. However, when a paddle stroke is applied properly, the paddle will move the canoe in the desired direction. So, don't try to overpower the canoe with brute force, instead, steer the canoe in the direction you want to go. The water pushing against the sides of a canoe weighs tons, and trying to overpower it is a mistake. Instead, use the canoe's momentum in the water and steer the boat with subtle paddle strokes to navigate in the direction you desire.

While a dozen or so strokes can be used to steer canoes, a combination of only three or four, when applied properly, is all that is needed to steer a canoe. Before I discuss the different strokes, let's talk about posture.

## Posture

If you have ever competed in sports, ridden a bicycle, taken dance lessons, or studied martial arts, you know that body position is all important. The same is true for canoeing. Experienced whitewater paddlers normally kneel in a canoe and get their center of gravity as low as possible to avoid tipping over. However, I normally sit on the seat while paddling. While I have knelt on occasion when paddling through rapids, all instructional tips and illustrations given in the following sections will demonstrate proper paddling technique while sitting in a canoe. I will briefly discuss the basic principles of kayak paddling later in this chapter.

When you sit in a canoe, it is important to sit up straight. This position allows you to see where you are going, and you will have more control over your paddle and more leverage when you perform a stroke. Sitting up straight also allows you to twist your torso and use the large muscles of the back and shoulders while paddling. Keep your feet spread about 18 inches apart with your knees slightly bent. If your canoe has footrests, place your feet on the footrests and apply a little pressure while paddling.

You may think that strong arms are needed to paddle, but the larger muscles of the shoulder, back, and upper torso are much stronger than your biceps, so twisting your torso with each stroke will allow you to paddle for hours without fatigue.

## Technique

To paddle efficiently, you will need to learn good technique. While traditional paddling instruction stressed paddling on only one side of the canoe and only rarely switching from side to side, I favor another technique that has been tested and refined by long distance paddlers and canoe racers. The method allows solo or tandem paddlers to switch the paddle from side to side frequently to steer the canoe. I will describe this technique in more detail later. I call it the "sit and switch" technique. It is sometimes referred to as the "Minnesota switch," pioneered by Gene Jensen. Known for his skill as a boatbuilder and expert canoe racer, Jensen learned that switching his paddle from side to side allowed him and his partner to steer a tandem canoe with forward strokes and still maintain the speed of the canoe. While you may have no desire to race or go fast, even so, learning all the strokes properly will allow you to choose which method you want to apply and to use the technique that works best for you.

Before you perform your first stroke, you need to know how to hold the paddle properly. I will start by describing proper hand position while paddling on the right side of the canoe. Begin by placing your left hand on the grip of the paddle. Hold it firmly and allow your wrist to be flexible, but not rigid since some of the strokes require subtle movement of the wrist to change the angle of the blade. Next, place your right hand on the shaft about 6 to 8 inches above the blade. If your paddle is too long, you may need to slide your right hand up the shaft toward the grip. Don't grip the paddle shaft too tightly, but it is important that you hold it firmly since your hand on the shaft guides the path of the paddle blade through the water. When you switch sides to paddle on the left side of the canoe, you will need to switch hand positions.

Once you have learned the different paddling strokes, you will realize that there are several different strokes that can be used in a given situation to steer the canoe. While some strokes are very effective, they also stop the canoe and compromise forward motion. As mentioned earlier, the "sit and switch" technique, in my opinion, is the most efficient technique to steer a canoe and still allow the canoe to move forward. In the following sections, I will discuss several different paddle strokes that will allow you to paddle your canoe in a straight line, turn right, turn left, or stop your canoe. I will focus primarily on paddle strokes and technique for paddling a tandem canoe (C-2). First, I will discuss several that I call "positive strokes."

## Forward Stroke

The forward stroke, as the name implies, is the stroke that is used to propel the canoe forward. This stroke is used the majority of the time and is used as long as the canoe is going in the desired direction. I call it a positive stroke because it moves the canoe in a forward direction. The movement is made up of four basic parts: the catch, power phase, exit, and recovery (fig. 5.1). I will discuss this stroke in great detail because several other strokes are simply a variation of this one, and learning it correctly will allow you to perform the others as well.

While the forward stroke can be performed on either side of the canoe, I will describe the technique for paddling on the left side (as shown in fig. 5.1). Performing the stroke on the right side of the canoe is simply a matter of switching your hand positions, and paddling on the right side.

Start by placing your right hand on the grip and your left hand on the shaft about 6 to 8 inches above the paddle blade. Once your hands are in the proper position, reach forward with the paddle on the left side of the canoe and slice the paddle into the water near the side of the canoe. As you reach forward, lower your left shoulder and keep your left (lower) arm almost straight. At the same time, bend your right arm slightly and keep your grip hand out in front of your face. Next, lower the paddle until the blade is submerged and keep the shaft as perpendicular to the surface of the water as possible. Make sure the blade is fully submerged before you start to pull on the paddle shaft. This is called the "catch" and is a very important part of the forward stroke.

Next, push down with your grip hand and pull straight back with the hand on the shaft. Because the bow and stern of a canoe narrow to a point, the placement

**FIGURE 5.1.** Joy demonstrates the four basic parts of the forward stroke.
Courtesy of Brad Belk

of the paddle differs slightly for the bow and stern paddlers. The bow paddler should place the paddle in the water about a foot out away from the gunwale, while the stern paddler should place the paddle in the water near the gunwale to begin the stroke. Don't follow the side of the canoe, but instead pull the paddle blade in a straight line parallel to the keel-line of the canoe. This is called the "power phase." While performing the power phase, twist your torso and use your back and shoulder muscles while pulling the blade back. When the paddle blade reaches your hip, you should drop your top hand that is on the grip and let the blade exit the water. This is called the "exit." Do not pull the blade past your hip because this pulls the canoe down, slows the canoe, and is counterproductive.

To begin another stroke, swing the paddle forward and slice the blade into the water. Returning the paddle to the starting position is called the "recovery." Many canoe instructional books describe the forward stroke and the recovery as forming a *D* in the water. While this is done to illustrate the correct path of the blade during the stroke and recovery, in truth, the blade is not pulled through the water but the canoe is pulled forward toward the paddle blade. To illustrate what actually happens when you perform the forward stroke, imagine a paddle that is permanently anchored in the water with the shaft sticking straight up vertically out of the water. If you were sitting in a canoe and you reached forward and placed one hand on the grip and the other hand on the shaft and pulled on the stationary paddle, your boat would move forward. This is actually what happens when you perform a forward stroke. The force exerted on the paddle blade is greater than the resistance of the canoe against the water. So the canoe moves forward in response to the laws of motion. The more effectively you can place the paddle in the water and perform a smooth "catch," the more efficiently the canoe moves forward. To recap, when you perform a forward stroke, your objective is to pull the canoe forward toward the blade. You must anchor (submerge) the blade before you begin to pull (power phase). To perform the paddle stroke on the opposite side of the canoe, simply switch sides during the recovery phase and switch your hand positions (fig. 5.2).

Before we move on to the next stroke, I want to stress the importance of learning the forward stroke properly. It is particularly important because this is the stroke that you use to move the canoe forward and it is used more than any other stroke. It is also the basis of several other strokes, so learning it correctly will make the others easier to learn.

*Tips to Make the Stroke More Effective*

If the forward stroke feels awkward at first, don't worry, it will get easier to perform if you practice. Also, there are a few things to keep in mind while performing the stroke.

- First, I can't overemphasize the importance of making the clean "catch" before you begin to pull on the paddle. If you pull on the paddle shaft (power phase) before you make the "catch," you will trap air between the blade and the water and the paddle will make noise and create turbulence. If the blade is not properly anchored in the water before you begin to pull on the paddle, the forward movement of the canoe will be compromised. So remember, slice the paddle blade in the water, make sure the paddle is submerged, hesitate momentarily,

**FIGURE 5.2.** Joy switching hand positions to paddle on the opposite side.
Courtesy of Brad Belk

and then begin the power phase. Practice this and you will learn to perform the catch smoothly.

- Next, during the power phase, keep the paddle shaft as vertical as possible. If the shaft is held vertical during the stroke, the canoe will move forward efficiently. Also, pull the blade straight back parallel to the keel-line of the canoe.
- Remember to pull on the paddle shaft until the blade is even with your hip and then pull the paddle out of the water. If you continue to pull the paddle past your hip, you will begin to pull the canoe down and not forward.
- The forward stroke can be used in the bow or stern of a tandem canoe and in a solo canoe as well.

Once you have learned to perform the forward stroke on the left side of the canoe, try a few strokes on the right side. After making several forward strokes on either side of a tandem canoe, the bow of the canoe will begin to veer away from the side the stern paddler is paddling on. The same is true for a paddler in a solo canoe. Why is this happening? Well, if you could stick your paddle straight down between your legs through the keel-line of the canoe and pull the paddle straight back under your seat, the canoe would go straight. However, since you are paddling along the side of the canoe and not directly along the keel-line, the craft will slowly veer away from the side the stern paddler is paddling on. When this happens, it is time to make a corrective or steering stroke.

## Draw Stroke

The "draw" is a steering stroke that is used to turn a canoe. Like the forward stroke, the draw will provide some forward motion while also steering. The degree to which the canoe turns depends upon the angle at which the stroke is applied. When the stroke is applied in the bow of a tandem canoe, the bow moves laterally to the side that the bow paddler is paddling on. When applied in the stern of a tandem canoe, the stern will move laterally to the side that the stern paddler is paddling on.

To illustrate the stroke, I will describe it when performed by the stern paddler in a tandem canoe. To begin the stroke, hold the paddle in the same way as the forward stroke, but instead of placing the paddle in the water and pulling the paddle parallel to the keel-line of the canoe, reach out away from the canoe forming a 45- to 60-degree angle with the keel-line and submerge the paddle in the water. Keep the paddle shaft as vertical as possible and pull the paddle in a straight line toward the side of the canoe and stop at your hip (fig. 5.3). Unlike the forward stroke, you have to use your arms and biceps to complete the stroke because it is difficult to twist your torso. Next, drop your grip hand and "exit" the paddle from the water and begin the recovery by reaching forward from the canoe to begin another stroke. If you are paddling in the stern and you want to make a more severe turn in the canoe, reach out away from your hip and submerge the paddle forming an 80- to 90-degree angle with the keel-line of the canoe and pull the blade toward the gunwale. It may take two, three, or more strokes before the canoe turns in the desired direction.

When the draw is used in the bow of a tandem canoe, the stroke will pull the bow to the side the paddler is paddling on (fig. 5.4). However, when the draw is applied in the stern, the stroke will pull the stern of the canoe to the side that the stern paddler is paddling on, and consequently, the bow of the canoe points to the side the bow paddler is paddling on (fig. 5.5). So, if you want to turn the canoe to the left, the stern paddler will perform draw strokes on the

FIGURE 5.3. Position of paddle at end of draw stroke for stern paddler (stop at hip). Courtesy of Brad Belk

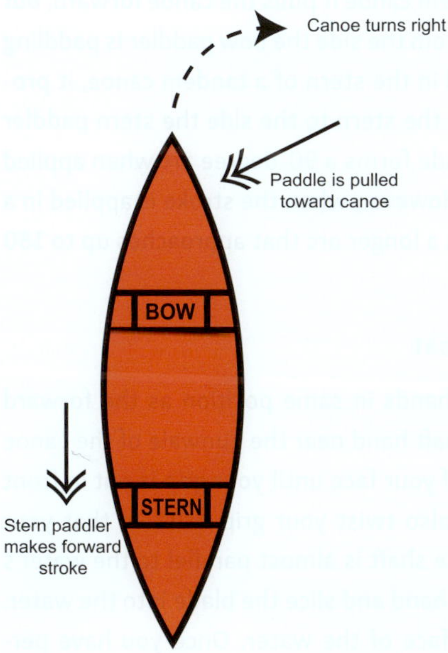


FIGURE 5.4. Bow draw on right; turns canoe right

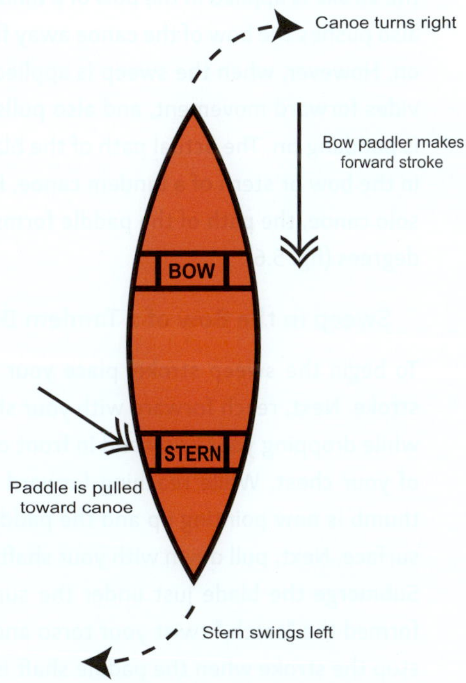


FIGURE 5.5. Stern draw on left; turns canoe right

right side of the canoe. The opposite is true for turning the canoe to the right. When the stroke is used in a solo canoe, because you are sitting in the center of the canoe, the stroke is less effective. While this stroke can be used in a solo canoe for steering, the sweep stroke, which will be described next, is used more frequently.

*Tips to Make the Stroke More Efficient*

- Reach out away from the side of the canoe and submerge the paddle fully, before you begin the draw stroke.
- Keep the paddle shaft vertical while performing the stroke.
- Exit the paddle when you reach your hip.
- The greater the angle of the draw stroke with the keel-line of the canoe, the more rapidly the canoe will turn.

## Sweep Stroke

Another stroke that is used to turn the canoe is the "sweep." The sweep is another positive stroke that steers the canoe but also moves it forward. The sweep is a variation of the forward stroke. It can be used in a tandem or solo canoe. When the stroke is applied in the bow of a tandem canoe it pulls the canoe forward, but also pushes the bow of the canoe away from the side the bow paddler is paddling on. However, when the sweep is applied in the stern of a tandem canoe, it provides forward movement, and also pulls the stern to the side the stern paddler is paddling on. The actual path of the blade forms a 90-degree arc when applied in the bow or stern of a tandem canoe. However, when the stroke is applied in a solo canoe, the path of the paddle forms a longer arc that approaches up to 180 degrees (fig. 5.6).

### Sweep in the Bow of a Tandem Boat

To begin the sweep stroke, place your hands in same position as the forward stroke. Next, reach forward with your shaft hand near the gunwale of the canoe while dropping your grip hand in front of your face until your grip is out in front of your chest. While reaching forward also twist your grip hand so that your thumb is now pointing up and the paddle shaft is almost parallel to the water's surface. Next, pull down with your shaft hand and slice the blade into the water. Submerge the blade just under the surface of the water. Once you have performed the "catch," twist your torso and pull the paddle in a 90-degree arc and stop the stroke when the paddle shaft is pointing perpendicular to the keel-line of the canoe. The stroke will push the bow of the canoe away from the side you are paddling on while also providing some forward motion (fig. 5.7).

*Tips to Make the Stroke More Effective*

Don't expect the sweep to immediately turn the canoe. It may take several sweep strokes for the bow to begin to drift in the desired direction.

- Remember to reach forward with your shaft hand and submerge the paddle blade just under the water's surface near the gunwale.
- Then, swing the blade out and away from the gunwale forming an arc. Stop the stroke when the shaft forms a 90-degree arc with the keel-line of the canoe.

## Sweep in the Stern of a Tandem Canoe

Generally speaking, the sweep is performed more frequently in the stern than in the bow of a tandem canoe. This is done primarily because the stern paddler calls the switches and his or her major function is to steer the canoe. The bow paddler can also steer the canoe, although the bow paddler's main function is to be the "motor" and move the canoe forward. So, if the stern paddler performs the sweep in the stern of the canoe, the stroke will provide some forward movement while also pulling the stern of the canoe to the same side that the paddler is paddling on.

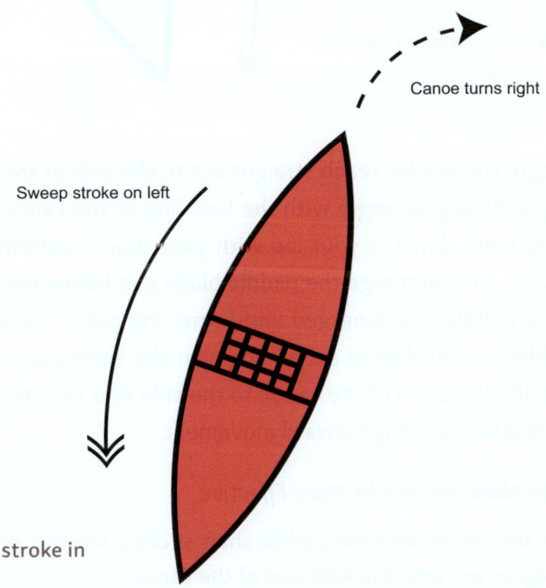


**FIGURE 5.6.** Sweep stroke in solo canoe

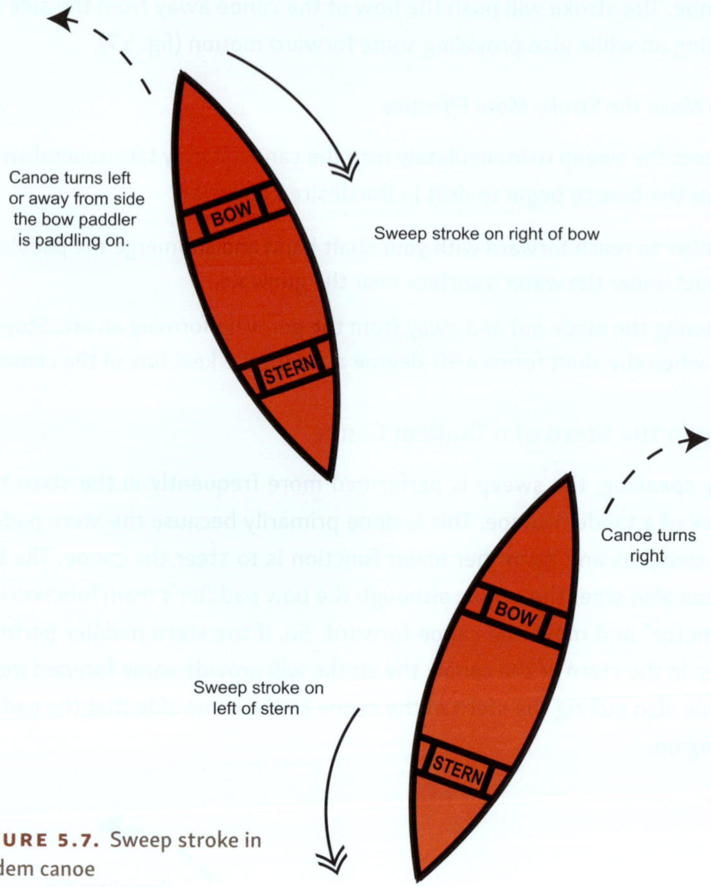


**FIGURE 5.7.** Sweep stroke in tandem canoe

To begin the stroke, reach straight out to the side of the canoe with the shaft forming a 90-degree angle with the keel-line of the canoe. Next, while keeping your grip hand down in your lap with your thumb pointing up, pull your shaft hand down and submerge the paddle blade just below the surface of the water. Once the paddle is submerged and forms the catch, twist your torso and pull the paddle in a 90-degree arc ending near the stern gunwale of the canoe. This stroke pulls the stern of the canoe to the side that the stern paddler is paddling on, while also providing forward movement.

*Tips to Make the Stroke More Effective*

- Begin the stroke with the paddle shaft sticking straight out forming a 90-degree arc with the keel-line of the canoe.

- Submerge the blade of the paddle in the water while holding your grip hand down in your lap with your thumb pointing up.
- Pull the blade through the water forming a 90-degree arc and stop the stroke when the blade reaches the gunwale.

When the sweep stroke is performed by both the stern paddler and the bow paddler while each is paddling on the same side of the canoe, the boat will turn faster.

The forward, sweep, and draw strokes, when applied properly, will allow you to move the canoe forward; additionally, the sweep and the draw will allow you make subtle corrections to the right or left as needed.

All three strokes use the muscles of the back, torso, and chest. However, the draw stroke also uses the biceps because the movement will not allow you to twist your torso. As mentioned earlier, I refer to these strokes as "positive" because they all move the canoe in a positive or forward direction.

Next I will describe several strokes that are very effective in turning the canoe but have a negative effect upon forward movement. These strokes slow and can even stop the canoe, and for that reason, I call them negative strokes.

## *J* Stroke

The *J* stroke has been taught by instructors for many years as a way to turn a canoe and has been described and emphasized in a number of canoe instructional manuals as the principle stroke for steering. The stroke is only used in the stern of a tandem canoe or a solo canoe and is favored especially by whitewater paddlers because you can paddle on one side of the canoe without needing to switch from side to side to steer. The stroke also allows you to keep the paddle in the water, which acts as an outrigger stabilizing the canoe. It is especially useful in turbulent or swift current because it allows you to keep your paddle in water to avoid capsizing. However, one negative aspect of the stroke is that it also slows the forward movement of the canoe.

The stroke is simply a forward stroke with a little different ending. To perform it, begin by making a forward stroke, but instead of stopping the paddle stroke at the hip continue to pull the paddle blade past the hip. Once your paddle passes your hip, twist your grip hand until your thumb is pointing down. Continue to drop your grip hand until the shaft is near the gunwale. In fact, you can even rest the shaft on the gunwale for leverage if you like. Make sure the blade is still submerged just below the water's surface and pull your grip hand across your lap while pushing the paddle blade out away from the canoe with your shaft hand (fig. 5.8). Once the power face of the blade begins to push against the water, the canoe will begin to pivot or turn toward the side the stern paddler is paddling on. Keep in mind that the blade acts as a rudder and will slow or stop the canoe if you continue to hold the *J* stroke in place. So the bow paddler should perform a forward stroke at the same time the stern paddler performs the *J* stroke. If you want to turn the canoe farther, continue to perform *J* strokes until the canoe is heading in the desired direction. Once the canoe is heading in the right direction, both bow and stern paddlers will begin to make several forward strokes until the canoe begins to drift away from the side that the stern paddler is paddling on. Then perform a few *J* strokes in the stern and you are back on track. By alternating between the forward stroke and the *J* stroke, the stern paddler in a tandem canoe or a solo paddler can steer the canoe forward and never have to switch the paddle from side to side. The *J* stroke can be used in a solo boat or in the stern of a tandem canoe.

*Tips to Make the Stroke More Effective*

- Perform a forward stroke, and then turn the thumb on your grip hand down before you start to pull your grip hand across your lap.
- Remember, while the stern paddler performs the *J* stroke, the bow paddler should perform forward strokes at the same time.
- The stroke works more effectively with a straight-shaft paddle because a bent-shaft paddle is bent in the wrong direction.

**FIGURE 5.8.** *J* stroke.
Courtesy of Brad Belk

## Rudder Strokes

In this section, I will describe several strokes that can be used to quickly turn or stop the canoe. The strokes are called "rudders," and as the name indicates, the strokes act just like a rudder. These moves are extremely effective because, like the *J* stroke, the rudder stroke uses the forward momentum of the canoe to turn the canoe. They also slow the forward motion of the canoe, and the strokes only work when the canoe is moving. Because the rudder stroke stops the movement of the canoe, it has a negative effect upon forward motion. First, I will discuss rudder strokes in the stern of a tandem canoe.

### Stern Rudder

The stern rudder is not a true stroke and is simply a maneuver. While it is the most effective method to turn the canoe, it has a negative effect upon the forward momentum of the canoe. Even if you have received no formal instruction, you will quickly learn that when you stick your paddle in the water in the stern of a tandem canoe that is moving, the canoe will turn quickly. The maneuver is used by more recreational paddlers to steer than any other. Here is how it is performed.

While sitting in the stern, place your hands in the forward stroke position and reach back behind your hip in the similar position as the *J* stroke, but keep the paddle blade just above the water. This time, keep your thumb pointed up, and raise your grip hand and lower your shaft hand until the paddle blade is submerged just below the water. Next, begin to pull your grip hand across your lap toward the keel-line of the canoe and push your shaft hand outward from the gunwale (fig. 5.9). You can gain added leverage by resting the shaft on the gunwale and applying leverage if you like. The stern rudder can be used by the stern paddler on the left side to turn left and on the right side to turn right. It can also be used in a solo canoe to turn the canoe in either direction.

*Tips to Make the Stroke More Effective*

- Slice the blade in the water near the side of the canoe just behind your hip and submerge the blade.
- Pull your grip hand across your lap and push away from the gunwale with your shaft hand.
- The boat must be moving before the rudder maneuver will work.

**FIGURE 5.9.** Stern rudder.

Courtesy of Brad Belk

## Bow Rudder or Post

The "bow rudder" or "post" is used by the bow paddler in a tandem canoe or it can be used in a solo canoe. The maneuver is called a "post" because when applied correctly, the paddle shaft sticks straight up out of the water like a "post" that is permanently anchored. To perform the stroke, begin by placing your hands on the paddle in the same positions as the forward stroke. Reach forward and slice the paddle blade in the water near the side of the canoe. As you reach forward, be sure to twist your grip hand so that your thumb is pointing toward your face and the paddle shaft is almost perpendicular to the water's surface (fig. 5.10). If you choose to reach farther forward to submerge the blade, you will need to drop your grip hand. As you slice the paddle blade in the water, make sure the paddle blade is almost parallel to the keel-line of the canoe. Once the paddle is submerged, begin to twist your grip hand so that the paddle blade creates a 20- to 45-degree angle with the keel-line of the canoe. Once you feel the force of the water pushing against the blade slowly turn your wrist to increase the angle of the blade, if needed. The greater the angle, the more force you will feel and the more the canoe will turn. Hold the rudder in place until the bow begins to turn.

Remember, the stern paddler will need to continue to paddle while the stroke is applied by the bow paddler or the canoe will stop. The post or bow rudder can also be used in a solo canoe.

*Tips to Make the Stroke More Effective*

- When the paddle blade is submerged, make sure the blade is parallel to the keel-line of the canoe.
- Slowly increase the angle of the blade with the keel until the canoe begins to turn.
- Hold the paddle firmly while performing the stroke since the force of the water pushing against the blade makes it difficult to hold.

## Cross Bow Rudder

The "cross bow rudder," or sometimes called the "cross bow draw," is also a steering stroke and can be used in a solo or tandem canoe. In a tandem canoe the stroke is only used in the bow. The move is very effective when an abrupt turn is needed. It is particularly useful when the bow paddler sees an obstruction in the water and needs to turn the canoe to avoid a collision.

**FIGURE 5.10.** Bow rudder or post.
Courtesy of Brad Belk

To begin the stroke, start with your hands in the forward stroke position with the paddle on the right side of the canoe. Without changing your hand positions, reach across the bow until the paddle blade is near the gunwale on the left side of the canoe just above the water. At the same time twist your grip hand until your thumb points up and the blade is parallel to the keel-line. I know this feels awkward, but you will learn that it is extremely effective when you need to make a quick, sharp turn. Next, pull your grip hand toward your chest and pull your shaft hand down until the blade is submerged below the water. Next, twist your grip hand until the blade forms a 20- to 45-degree angle with the keel-line of the canoe (fig. 5.11). If you want to turn the canoe farther, simply increase the angle of the blade by pulling the grip hand farther across your lap while pushing out away from the canoe with your shaft hand. As you increase the angle of the blade with the keel-line of the canoe, the canoe will turn faster, but the force of the water pushing against the blade makes it increasingly difficult to hold the paddle in place. Also, if you increase the angle of the paddle blade while paddling briskly it may almost launch you out of your canoe. One tip for holding the stroke in place is to position the shaft against the top of the gunwale and hold it in place with your shaft hand.

**FIGURE 5.11.** Bob demonstrates a cross bow rudder.
Courtesy of Brad Belk

*Tips to Make the Stroke More Effective*

- When you insert the blade in the water, keep the blade near the gunwale and open the power face slowly.
- If you open up the power face, creating a 90-degree angle with the keel-line of the canoe, you will turn the canoe abruptly and can even stop the canoe.

## Back or Reverse Stroke

The last stroke I will discuss is the back or reverse stroke. It is a very effective way to stop or slow your canoe and can be used in the bow or the stern of a tandem canoe or in a solo canoe. It is the reverse of the forward stroke and is often used when launching or docking your canoe or when you want to stop your canoe or move it backward to avoid obstacles that are directly in your path.

To begin the stroke, simply hold the paddle as if you were going to perform a forward stroke on the left side of the canoe. Next rotate your torso toward the left side of the canoe and submerge your paddle blade in the water just behind your hip. At the same time, drop your grip hand and align the paddle shaft parallel to the keel-line of the canoe. Push down and forward with your shaft hand, pull back and up on your grip hand and push the blade forward in a straight line parallel to the keel-line of the canoe. Stop the stroke once it passes your hip and repeat the stroke if needed (fig. 5.12). Be careful when you apply the stroke in

**FIGURE 5.12.** Joy's blade entering the water for a back or reverse stroke.
Courtesy of Brad Belk

a moving canoe because the moving canoe has inertia, and when you insert the paddle blade in the water to begin the stroke, the force of the water on the blade can force the paddle out of your hands. The stroke will feel very awkward at first, but you will learn to perform it with practice. Remember, if you are paddling with a bent-shaft paddle, you will need to rotate the paddle 180 degrees before you begin the stroke. Why? Well, unless you rotate the bent-shaft paddle blade, the blade will not make a smooth catch and will cavitate in the water.

*Tips to Make the Stroke More Effective*

- Make sure your blade is pulled in a straight line parallel to the keel-line of the canoe.

## Other Strokes

While there are a number of other strokes that can be used to steer a canoe, by using those described above you will be able to steer with all the control and efficiency you normally need. If you want to learn other strokes or paddle whitewater, there are several books that you may want to read. Bill Mason, highly regarded whitewater paddler, outdoorsman, and author, has several books and videos on whitewater paddling. His book, *Path of the Paddle* (1995), describes and illustrates many different whitewater strokes. Also, if you want to learn the proper technique and subtle nuances of strokes used in canoe racing, read Peter Heed's book *Canoe Racing* (2004).

### Sit and Switch Technique

I mentioned earlier that I prefer the "sit and switch" technique of steering a tandem canoe. The method has several advantages compared to constantly using negative strokes in the stern to turn the canoe. However, the sit and switch technique takes some time and practice to master. It allows you to cover more distance in your canoe, and the canoe will move more smoothly through the water when both tandem paddlers use this technique. It can also be used to steer a solo canoe. See Textbox 3 for an exercise that will improve your "sit and switch" technique.

Next, I will describe the technique for paddling a tandem boat. Because the bow and stern paddlers have different responsibilities, I will describe the role of each paddler separately.

### Bow Paddler

The bow paddler is responsible for setting the pace or stroke rate, and he or she begins by performing a forward stroke. The bow paddler is sometimes referred to as the "motor" as his or her primary function is to propel the canoe forward, but he or she can also provide corrective strokes to help steer. Since the torso of the bow paddler often blocks the view of the stern paddler, the bow paddler must look for submerged rocks, logs, or other obstacles directly in front of the canoe and must make quick maneuvers such as draws or cross bow draws when needed to prevent a collision and possible unplanned swim.

The stern paddler simply paddles at the same time as the bow paddler. Once the bow paddler has begun to paddle the forward stroke, the stern paddler will perform a forward stroke at the same time, but on the opposite side of the canoe. Both paddlers will continue to paddle the forward stroke until the stern paddler gives instructions to perform another stroke or to switch sides and paddle on the opposite side of the canoe.

### Stern Paddler

The stern paddler's principle responsibility is to steer the canoe, and since he or she sits directly behind the bow paddler and can watch the stroke rate, it is easy to follow the same paddle cadence as the bow paddler. Once the canoe begins to move forward, and after several strokes, the bow of the canoe will normally begin to drift to the side that the bow paddler is paddling on. This occurs because the stern paddler's stroke tends to pull the canoe stern laterally to the side that the stern paddler is paddling on. To correct the path of the canoe, two things must happen. First, the stern paddler must tell the bow paddler to switch sides and begin to perform the forward stroke on the opposite side of the canoe. I use the simple command, "hut" to signal the bow paddler to switch sides. At the same time the stern paddler will also switch sides and start to perform a forward stroke or corrective stroke on the opposite side if needed. If the switch is made at precisely the right time, only a forward stroke may be needed. However, if the canoe has begun to drift too far in the wrong direction before the switch is made, then the stern paddler will perform a draw stroke or two as needed. Once the canoe begins to head in the right direction, both paddlers will continue to make forward strokes in unison until the canoe begins to drift off course. When this happens, the stern paddler will call another "hut," and the bow paddler will switch sides and the stern paddler will begin to make forward strokes or possibly

## Paddling in a Straight Line

While you may be content to only drift leisurely along in your canoe and make an occasional stern rudder or *J* stroke to steer, by switching sides and using the draw or sweep strokes, your canoe will move faster and smoother through the water. If you want to hone your skills and improve your paddling technique, try the "sit and switch" technique.

To teach new paddlers to learn this technique, I ask them to try to paddle their canoe in a straight line. Why a straight line? Well, when you learn to paddle "in a straight line," you actually learn to maneuver your boat because you are constantly steering so that the bow is heading in the right direction. As I mentioned earlier, canoes, especially recreational ones, tend to drift from side to side. This occurs because the bottom of the canoe is relatively flat and the bottom of the stern and bow sit higher in the water than the center of the boat. When you paddle the canoe, it tends to move to the right or left as the bow and stern slide across the water. When you learn to steer the canoe with the "sit and switch" technique, you will learn to switch paddle strokes frequently to steer. The "sit and switch" technique will allow you to go farther and faster, and you can impress your friends with your skill and prowess in a canoe.

One way to perfect the technique is to pick a feature in the water, or on the bank, in front of your canoe and position the boat so that it points toward the feature. Imagine that there is a line that runs from the bow of your canoe to the feature. To begin, the bow paddler will paddle a forward stroke and the stern paddler will also paddle the forward stroke, but on the opposite side of the canoe. Again, both paddlers should paddle at the same time. After a few strokes, the bow of the canoe will begin to swing off course, toward the side that the bow paddler is paddling on. When this occurs, the stern paddler will need to call a "switch" or "hut," and both paddlers will switch sides. The bow paddler will continue to perform forward strokes while the stern paddler begins to make subtle draw strokes. After a few strokes, the canoe should begin to stop drifting away from the imaginary line and start to swing back toward the line. Once the bow of the canoe begins to swing back toward the line, another switch by both paddlers will be needed. Both paddlers will continue to switch from side to side as needed, to keep the canoe moving, and to keep it pointed in the right direction. At first this will seem difficult, because recreational canoes have lots of "rocker" and the canoe will drift from side to side. Learning at precisely the right time to call the switch is the key to keeping the canoe pointing in the right direction. With practice, you can become more proficient at steering your canoe. Because the stern paddler is the one responsible for calling the "switches" and knowing when to perform draw strokes, the stern paddler's task can be difficult. It may be frustrating at first because the canoe does not want to move in a straight line.

**FIGURE 5.13.** Stern paddler technique / paddling in a straight line

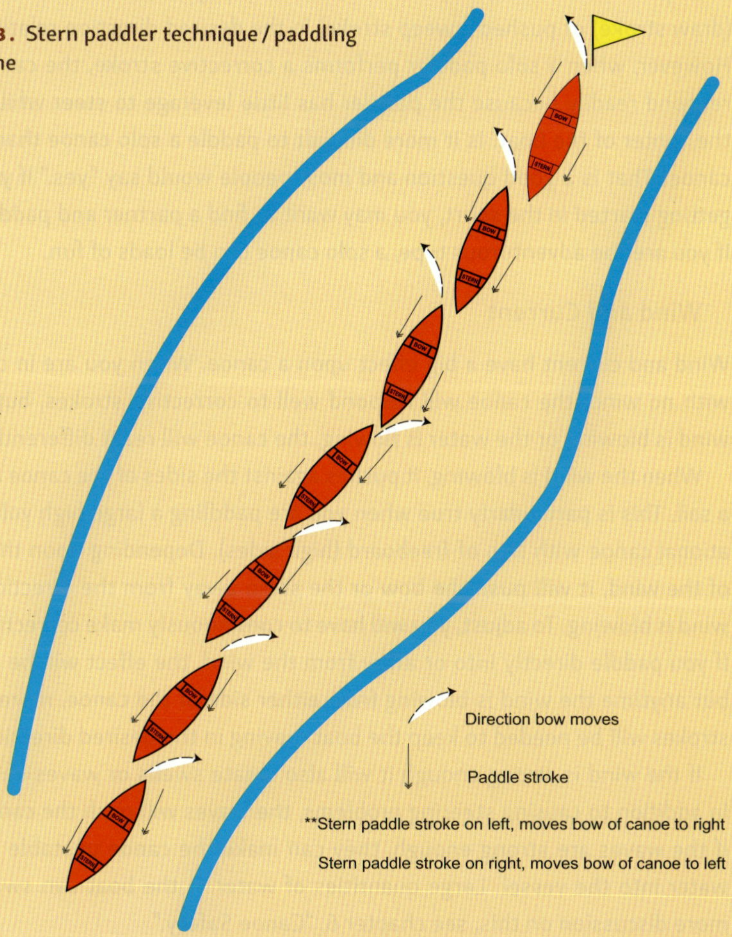

another stroke such as a draw or sweep if a correction is needed immediately. This technique may seem difficult in the beginning, but with practice, the technique will become easier.

## Paddling a Solo Canoe

While all the strokes previously described are useful in a solo canoe, there are a few other things to consider. Since you don't have a partner to help steer the canoe, you are all on our own. You don't have anyone to help avoid an obstruction in the water, and you don't have anyone to blame but yourself if the canoe doesn't go where you want.

When you sit in a solo canoe, you are positioned in the center of the canoe. In a tandem canoe there are paddlers in both ends of the canoe. When tandem paddlers perform a stroke, because of the laws of physics, the canoe can be pulled (draw stroke) or pushed (sweep stroke) in the desired direction relatively easily. However, when a solo paddler performs a corrective stroke, the canoe will not respond readily because the paddler has little leverage to steer while sitting in the center of the boat. Is it more difficult to paddle a solo canoe than a tandem canoe? That is a good question and most people would say "yes." If you are just getting started in the sport, you may want to find a partner and paddle tandem. If you are the adventurous type, a solo canoe can be loads of fun.

## Wind and Current

Wind and current have a big effect upon a canoe. When you are in quiet water with no wind, the canoe will respond well to corrective strokes, but when the wind is blowing or the water is flowing, the canoe will react differently.

When the wind is blowing, it pushes against the sides of the canoe and acts as a sail. This is particularly true when you are paddling a large high volume recreational canoe with lots of freeboard (high sides). Depending upon the direction of the wind, it will push the bow or the stern away from the direction that the wind is blowing. To adjust, you will have to continuously make corrective strokes. If you paddle directly into or away from the wind, the effect will be minimized, but anytime the wind is blowing from either side of the canoe, more corrective strokes will be needed to keep the boat moving in the desired direction.

If the wind is strong enough it will also create swells or waves on the water. In addition to causing steering problems, the waves will push the canoe around. If the waves are strong enough, they can make the canoe unstable and splash water into the vessel. Large quantities of water in the boat can swamp it. For more discussion on this, see chapter 6, "Canoe Safety."

If you plan to paddle on a fast-flowing stream, your ability to control the canoe will be affected. While I will not attempt to describe whitewater maneuvers for paddling in swift current, I will provide a few tips that will aid you when paddling in current. Paddling downstream, the current pushes on the stern of the canoe. As long as you keep the boat straight with the current, it is easy to control. However, when you have to make a turn to follow the river, the current will push against the stern of the canoe and turn the boat abruptly. To avoid making a 180-degree turn, several draw strokes in the stern and/or bow can keep the canoe on course.

## Let's Talk about Trim

Weight distribution can affect steering. I have heard horror stories from novice paddlers who insist that they simply cannot steer their canoe. I certainly understand, and while inexperience can be a contributing factor, I think I know a likelier problem: the canoe's trim. "Trim" is a term used to describe how level the canoe sits in the water. If the weight in the bow or stern is heavier than the weight in the opposite end of the canoe, how the canoe handles will be greatly affected. If there is too much weight in the bow, the canoe will tend to plow through the water and will be difficult to steer. Conversely, if the canoe is carrying too much weight in the stern, it will weave from side to side and constantly need steering corrections. Shifting gear in the canoe to balance (trim) the boat can correct the problem (fig. 5.14). Some touring canoes and most racing canoes have seats that are resting on cylinder tubes, which allow you to slide the seat forward or backward to trim the canoe.

## Kayak Paddling

While the intent of this chapter is to discuss the proper technique for paddling a canoe, I do want to discuss briefly kayak paddling and pass along a few observations. If you own a kayak, you already know it differs from a canoe in several ways. Unlike canoes, traditional kayaks have a deck that covers the top of the boat, with a cockpit to sit in. Surf skis and sit-on-tops have decks that cover the entire top surface of the boat, making them unsinkable. Because kayaks have less volume than canoes, paddlers sit lower in the water and have a lower center of gravity. Therefore, recreational kayaks are generally more stable than canoes. For all these reasons, kayaks are the choice of whitewater paddlers.

Also, plastic recreational kayaks are generally the first choice for young and beginner paddlers because kayaks are less expensive, are durable, and last for years. While some kayaks have storage areas, many do not. Kayaks cannot carry

a

b

**FIGURE 5.14** a and b. Photos of a boat that is not in trim (*a*) and a boat that is trimmed (*b*). Courtesy of Sandy Yonley

larger ice chests, camping gear, food, clothing, and other cargo for longer river trips or overnight stays. Canoes are a better choice if you plan to carry lots of gear.

While both canoes and kayaks are paddle driven, canoe and kayak paddles differ significantly. Kayak paddles are longer than canoe paddles and have a blade on each end of a cylindrical shaft. To paddle a kayak, you simply twist your torso and use your arms to guide the paddle through the water. By alternating your stroke from side to side and pulling with equal resistance during each stroke, you can steer your kayak in the direction you desire. If you want to turn your kayak, you simply pull harder on one side and the kayak will slide across the water to the opposite side from the one you are paddling on. The paddle stroke is also faster than the canoe stroke, because you don't have to switch the paddle from side to side. Also, when you swing your paddle forward during the "recovery" phase of the stroke, you are simultaneously performing the "power" phase on the opposite side of the kayak. Consequently, racing kayaks are faster than racing canoes. If a kayak is your choice of a paddle craft, there are videos and books that give instructional tips on all the paddle strokes. If you choose to paddle a coastal paddling trail, where winds and waves could swamp your boat, I would recommend a kayak.

# 6 Canoe Safety

Canoeing is a wonderful sport that provides many hours of pleasure. However, it is important to remember that the sport can be dangerous. Knowing your abilities is the first rule of safe canoeing. Always err on the side of safety: "it is better to be safe than sorry."

As a rule, it is safer to paddle with a partner or paddle with other boats. Certainly, you may choose to paddle alone, but if you are injured or have a medical problem you have no one to come to your aid. Whether you are just out for a short paddle, or you are leaving for a canoe camping trip that may last several days, it is important to plan for the unexpected. Good planning can prevent many of the problems that you may encounter. There are three important factors that you should consider: clothing, equipment, and conditions. Are you dressed properly and do you have an extra set of clothes in case you take an unscheduled swim? Do you have an extra paddle? Do you have plenty of water and/or food for your trip? Have you checked the weather? Are daily temperatures above 90 degrees or, are air and water temperatures both below 50 degrees? These are all things you should consider to ensure a safe trip on the water.

Over the past thirty years, I have paddled in all types of weather and water conditions, and I have been in a few unsafe situations that could have been avoided had I planned properly and taken the right equipment and clothing. I recall one trip in the fall when my wife, Joy, and I went paddling on the Guadalupe River. We were on a stretch of the river that is now the Victoria Paddling Trail. The weather was cool but not cold, and since it was supposed to warm up, I only wore biking shorts, a t-shirt, ball cap, and river shoes. Joy tends to run cold, so she wore nylon tights, a long-sleeved fleece top, and a vest. We were planning to make a day of it and had plenty of water and a snack, but no change of clothes. We put-in at the Highway 236 crossing of the Guadalupe River near Cuero, which is approximately 40 miles from the take-out at the boat ramp in Victoria City Park. Unfortunately, I did not check the weather forecast again before our trip. Everything went well for the first few hours, but then the weather turned. I could see large clouds rolling in, the wind began to blow, and the temperature dropped. A light rain started to fall, and since we were only a few miles from our take-out, we decided to continue. I did not have my GPS receiver, so I did not know the exact distance to the end, but we were accustomed to paddling long river stretches, and we thought we could make it. We had arranged for a friend to pick us up at the take-out, and he would be expecting us soon.

As we paddled, the temperature kept dropping and the rain continued to fall. We picked up our pace to keep warm and get to the end. By this time, I was soaked (did I mention my t-shirt was cotton?), but I felt I could continue. Joy, who had dressed properly, was fine. As we paddled, the wind continued to blow and the rain poured down. The temperature was maybe 60 degrees, but the strong winds plus the rain made it feel much colder to me. Although I paddled at a brisk pace, I started to have worsening chills. I began to shiver so badly I couldn't speak clearly. I had never been so cold before.

Worried, we took-out to warm up, but there was no tree cover nearby so we huddled close together for warmth. Finally, I took off the wet cotton t-shirt that was soaked through, and after a while I slowly stopped shivering. By this time, the rain and wind subsided. I felt better, so we decided to put-in and paddled to the end. After about ten minutes, we reached our take-out, where my friend had parked our car. Thankfully, I had left dry clothes inside. After changing, I turned on the car heater and just sat in the warmth for a while. In hindsight, the situation was easily preventable if I had done my due diligence: checked the weather conditions, worn warmer clothing, and taken along a rain top and some extra clothes in the canoe. While this is the first time I had actually experienced mild hypothermia, it taught me a lesson. See "Hypothermia" later in this chapter.

I hope you will take my advice and plan and prepare properly. Listed below are a few tips to consider before you go paddling to make your trip a safer one:

- Plan a paddling trip that will allow plenty of time for you to reach your destination. Plan to be off the water before dark.
- Don't paddle on water that you are not familiar with unless you go with someone who is knowledgeable, or talk with others about the area to learn about any safety hazards, such as rapids, portages, rocks, strong currents, and other obstructions.
- Make sure you have a car parked at the take-out, have someone meet you at the end, or have a canoe livery provide a shuttle to your car.
- Take a white light, whistle, or other signaling device to use if you have an emergency.

- Carry a US Coast Guard approved life jacket (PFD) for each paddler in your boat. A PFD is required by state law while canoeing or kayaking. *Wearing* the jacket is recommended. The jacket can also keep you warm in an emergency.
- Always check the weather before you go out. This is particularly important when you are planning a longer river trip or paddling on lakes or coastal waters. Heavy rain or winds can cause hazardous conditions.
- Where possible, paddle with other boats. The camaraderie is great, and if there is a medical emergency, other boats can provide assistance or go for help.
- Take along a cell phone or radio to call for help if needed.
- Always carry a spare paddle. A paddle can break or can drop into the water, unable to be retrieved.
- Tell someone where you plan to paddle and let them know that you will call them when you get off the water.
- Always carry plenty of food and water. You never know when you might have a problem and need to be on the water longer than planned.
- Take along a change of clothes. It may rain or you may take an unplanned swim.
- Scout obstacles in the river: low water dams, log jams, rocks, low hanging limbs, and such. Remember, "When in doubt, take-out."
- Secure all items in your canoe with a river strap, rope, or carabiner. If your boat capsizes, unsecured equipment will be lost.
- If you are paddling with a group and you have experienced paddlers along, let them lead the group.
- Make a list of equipment needs before your trip and check the list before you leave. A list of items to take along when canoeing is shown in appendix 1.
- Take along a GPS receiver to track your progress.

## Hyperthermia and Hypothermia

Someone once said, "If you don't like Texas weather, wait a little while and it will change." I have experienced this on more than one occasion. Hot summer days in Texas, when daily temperatures exceed 100 degrees, or sudden cold fronts in late fall and winter can change an otherwise enjoyable canoe trip into an unpleasant and even serious situation. Proper planning as mentioned earlier is important. Being properly dressed for a canoe or kayak trip and having a change of clothes is recommended. In cold weather, extra clothes will keep you warm if you capsize or if a Texas cold front catches you off guard, you can add an extra layer of clothing. Being too hot or too cold when you are miles from the take-out can be a serious problem. When the weather is cooler and the air temperature and water temperature are each less than 50 degrees, care should be taken to avoid a condition known as hypothermia.

### Hypothermia

Hypothermia occurs when your body's core temperature drops to the point where your muscles and/or brain function are impaired. The condition can occur from prolonged exposure to cold air temperatures, and/or exposure to water. It does not have to be a day when the air temperature is freezing or below. In fact, temperatures in the 50-degree range accompanied by getting wet can cause serious problems if you capsize or get caught unprepared in a rain shower. Since the best way to avoid the condition is to plan for the unexpected, following the tips listed below will help prevent the condition.

If you or someone in your party begins shivering, has slurred speech, or has impaired muscle function, he or she may be experiencing hypothermia. If the condition worsens, the affected person can shiver violently and may express erratic behavior.

If you are canoeing and your partner or someone in your party exhibits these symptoms, you should dock your boat and get on dry land. If there is shelter nearby, get out of the wind and/or rain. If the affected person's clothes are wet, remove them and get him or her to put on dry, warm clothing. Wrap the affected person in a survival blanket or sleeping bag, if available.

If the person seems to recover and begins to warm up and feel better, make sure he or she has recovered sufficiently before continuing the trip. However, if the conditions worsen, with severe shivering, more slurred speech, and confusion or unusual behavior, you should seek help immediately.

### Hyperthermia

Being too hot for an extended period and not taking in enough fluids on hot days can cause a serious medical condition known as heat exhaustion or hyperthermia. Obvious precautions such as wearing light clothing, a hat or cap, and drinking water and electrolyte supplements are recommended. Taking a dip in the water and finding a shady spot to rest are also ways to cool off. There are several warning signs of heat exhaustion that you should look out for, such as profuse sweating, muscle cramps, headache, nausea, dizziness, and elevated heart rate.

Should the symptoms of heat exhaustion occur, it is important to cool off by finding a shady place, stop paddling, get in the water or wet your clothing, drink water and/or an electrolyte drink, and rest. If the symptoms persist you should seek medical help.

## Portaging and Private Property

While all Texas paddling trails are on public waters, the majority of the land that borders the trails is private. In fact, according to the US Census Bureau, an estimated 96 percent of Texas is privately owned. Unless you are paddling through a state park, wildlife management area, or other state or federal lands, the banks of the river are private property and off limits unless you have been given permission by the landowner to enter the property. That does bring up one interesting question: "What should I do when an obstacle in the river causes an unsafe condition and I need to portage?" I know from practical experience that portaging to avoid an obstruction is a common practice, and the laws on navigating waterways can be confusing. The Texas Parks and Wildlife Department website (http://tpwd.texas.gov/fishboat/boat/paddlingtrails/) advises:

> As part of the navigation right, one may use the bed of a navigable stream, however, climbing out onto the banks can be considered trespassing. Criminal trespass occurs when one goes onto property after receiving notice not to enter. Notice includes verbal notice, a fence, sign(s), the presence of purple paint on posts or trees, or the visible presence of crops grown for human consumption. When encountering an obstruction in the riverbed, one has the right to portage around the obstruction, but take a direct path around and return to the streambed without lingering on the bank.

# 7 Texas Waters and History of State Paddling Trails Program

With fifteen major river systems and more than 191,000 miles of streams, Texas has a vast river network that crisscrosses the landscape (fig. 7.1). Because rainfall in the state increases as you move east, the land transitions from the Chihuahuan Desert in the west to swamps and pine forests in the east. From the western arid Trans Pecos desert country where the Rio Grande separates Texas from Mexico, to the Pineywoods in East Texas where the Sabine River forms the boundary with Louisiana, rivers define the character of the land and are major factors influencing population growth.

In addition to a vast river network, Texas also has more inland water than any other state except Minnesota, "the land of 10,000 lakes."[1] Texas has many man-made lakes that were created by damming streams, but Caddo Lake is generally recognized as the only natural lake. Located near Texas' eastern border with Louisiana, Caddo Lake is one of the most diverse in the state. Known for its many swampy areas and magnificent bald cypress trees, this 26,800-acre lake is a paradise for bird life and many other wildlife species (fig. 7.2).[2] Last but not least, Texas' coastal bays and inlets along the Gulf of Mexico form a continuous waterway that stretches 367 miles. With its rivers, lakes, and coastal bays, Texas truly can be a water wonderland.

Human development on the landscape has greatly modified and often diminished the natural beauty of land along riverbanks, but rivers remain sought-after resources that provide many hours of pleasure and recreation to outdoor enthusiasts. While canoes are no longer a major means of transportation, they still provide a source of recreation for thousands, a fitness program for some, and for others like myself, a lifelong passion.

During the 1990s, paddle sports were listed as one of the top five sports in growth, and by 1999, estimates reveal that approximately three million North Americans owned canoes, kayaks, and rowboats.[3] In 1996, a Texas survey revealed that an estimated 8 percent of the population, or approximately 1.5 million Texans, went canoeing, kayaking, or rafting during the year.[4] The survey also revealed that more than 735,000 Texans owned paddleboats. Since the original survey, the popularity of paddle sports has continued to grow across the nation. A recent survey titled "2015 Special Report on Paddlesports" (2015) conducted by the Outdoor Foundation estimates that 21.7 million, or 7.4 percent of the US population, paddled canoes, kayaks, or other paddle craft. The data also show that the thirteen-to-seventeen and eighteen-to-twenty-four age groups are the fastest-growing paddle age groups. Based upon my observations on the Lady Bird Lake Paddling Trail in Austin, this is particularly true for SUP paddlers.

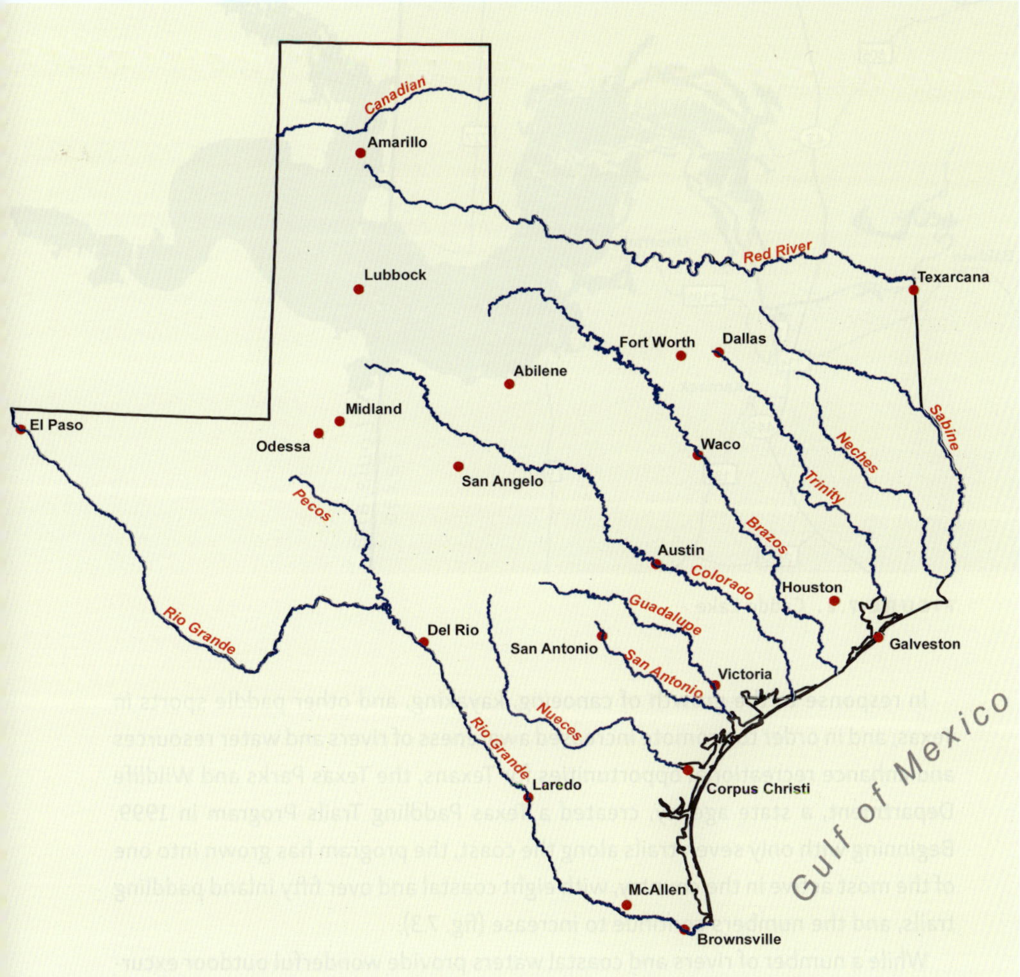


**FIGURE 7.1.** Major Texas rivers

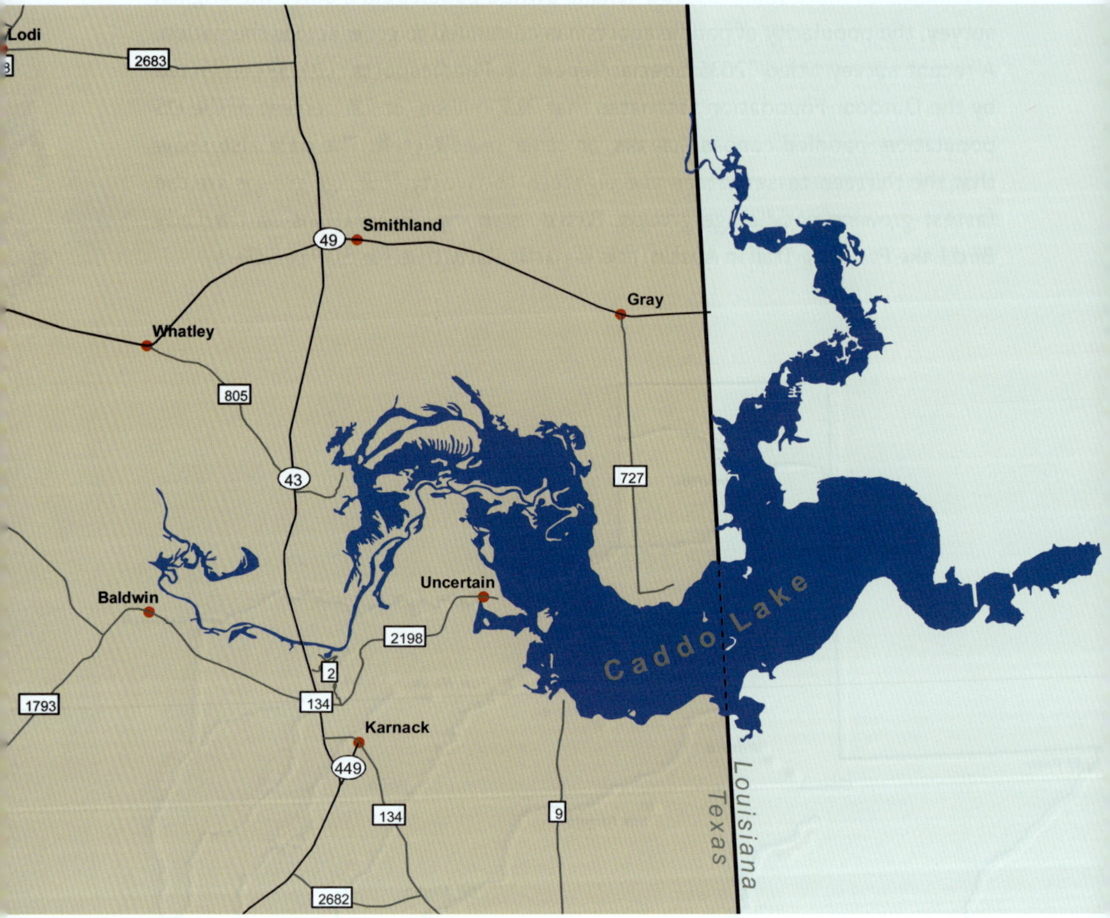


**FIGURE 7.2.** Caddo Lake

In response to the growth of canoeing, kayaking, and other paddle sports in Texas, and in order to promote increased awareness of rivers and water resources and enhance recreational opportunities for Texans, the Texas Parks and Wildlife Department, a state agency, created a Texas Paddling Trails Program in 1999. Beginning with only seven trails along the coast, the program has grown into one of the most active in the country, with eight coastal and over fifty inland paddling trails, and the numbers continue to increase (fig. 7.3).

While a number of rivers and coastal waters provide wonderful outdoor excursions, I will discuss the state's Paddling Trails Program and also provide some basic information on a few of my favorites (see chapter 8). I hope that you will

## Drought

Over the last three years I have traveled the state and paddled hundreds of miles on the state's paddling trails. Because of drought conditions, I encountered a few unexpected surprises when I arrived at a trail's put-in. During 2014 and 2015, I traveled to several lakes where the water level had receded to a point where portions of the trails could not be paddled. One paddling trail was completely dry, and several others were on lakes that were so low that the put-in had receded to the point where it was too far to carry my boat to launch. Also, I learned that local man-made changes can affect paddling trails. For example, I traveled to one trail that was in an urban area where a large interstate highway construction project had blocked the put-in. Reportedly, the project would not be completed for two years or more. While it appears that recent rains have filled many reservoirs and the drought may be over, I would advise that you always check with the Texas Parks and Wildlife Department, or better still, contact the local sponsor(s) listed on the TPWD website to learn the condition of any trail you intend to paddle. Also, take along some friends when you paddle. Aside from the safety aspect, it makes shuttling vehicles to the take-out easier.

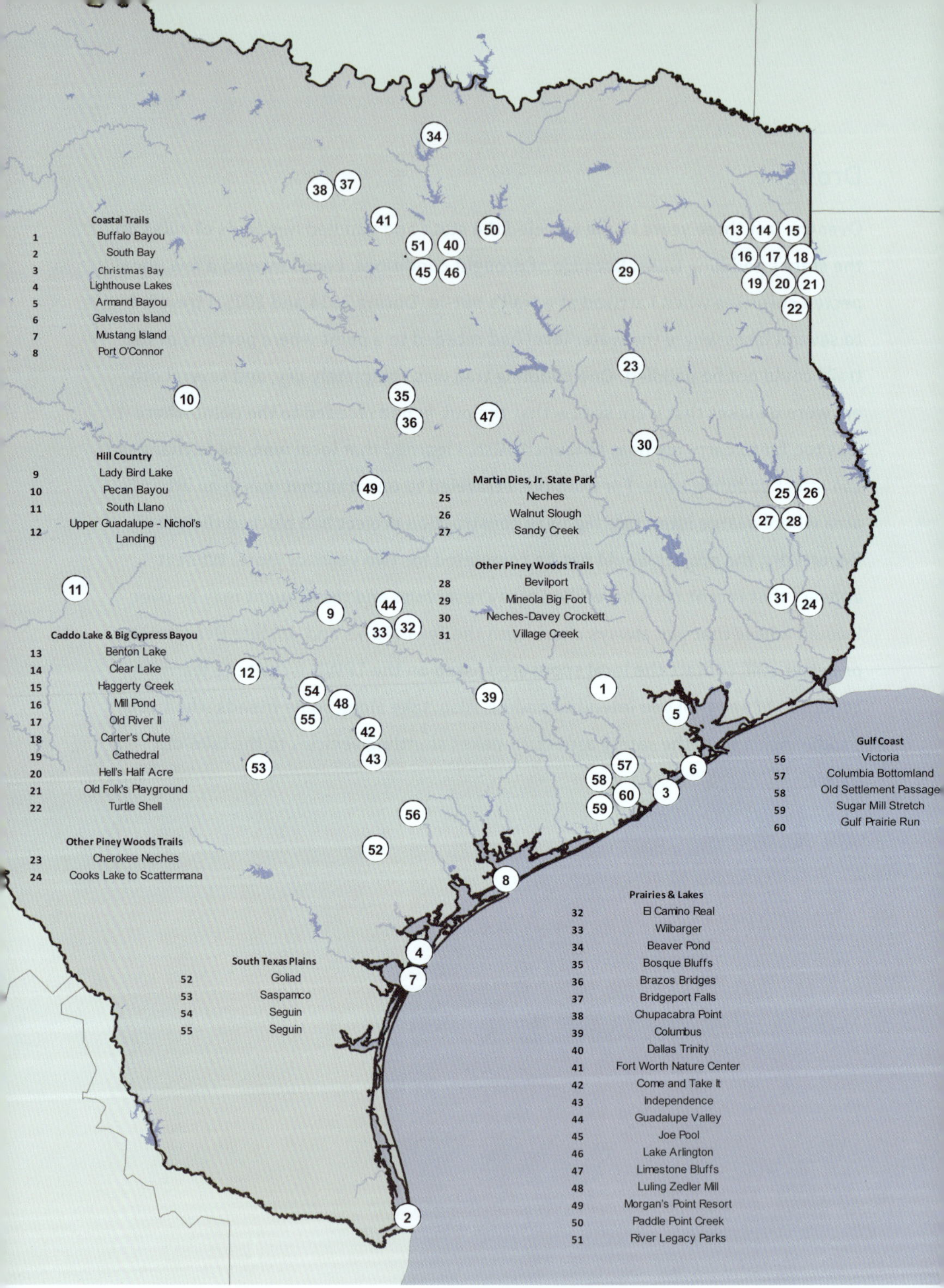


**FIGURE 7.3.** Map of Texas showing location of the paddling trails

embrace the sport of canoeing and get out and see for yourself how exciting and enjoyable Texas waterways and paddling can be.

Not only in Texas but also across the nation, paddling trails and "blueways," as they are called in some states, are growing in numbers. Information developed by the American Canoe Association reveals all fifty states have paddling trails or blueways and that there are more than one thousand trails nationwide. While paddling trails programs may differ from state to state, they all have a common goal: to provide information and access to outdoor excursions and open up paddle ways for people to explore. Whether you want to get back to nature, get a little exercise, or just get away from the hustle and bustle of your daily life, there is something invigorating about paddling down a flowing river, stream, lake, or coastal bay. There is truly magic in that feeling of pulling your paddle against the water and feeling your boat glide effortlessly across it. This experience can truly be life changing to those who choose to try it. I must admit, I am one of those.

## How State Paddling Trails Are Created

Here is how a river, stream, or lake becomes a state paddling trail. First, a local community partner/sponsor (a public entity) approaches the Texas Parks and Wildlife Department with a proposal to create a paddling trail. The department then informs the sponsor of what is needed to establish a trail, and the sponsor then submits an application. In some cases, the community partner submits an application prior to approaching the department, which is also acceptable. If the application has all the required parameters, the department will begin to coordinate with the applicant and develop needed information about the trail. After further evaluation and if there is a firm commitment by the applicant, the Texas Parks and Wildlife Department will begin to investigate the proposed trail. The department will perform a survey of the waterway to evaluate features along the trail, determine the length of the trail, and map the trail and pertinent access points with a Geographic Positioning System (GPS) receiver. As the planning process proceeds, the department will continue to provide technical support, while the local sponsor works to establish access points with sufficient parking and works with the Texas Department of Transportation to install directional signage along roadways leading to the trail. Signage for the trail is provided to the community partner by the department, but the community partner is responsible for installing the signs.

In addition to directional signs that are installed along roadways to locate each paddling trail, kiosks are installed to provide pertinent information about each trail. Kiosks are interpretive signs that are placed at the start (put-in) and end (take-out) of each trail. Each kiosk has a map, GPS coordinates, information about the trail, emergency telephone numbers, and other pertinent information about the trail. Some of the trails such as those in coastal waters, Caddo Lake, and some waterways may also have numbered trail markers and other directional signs along the trail.

As the planning proceeds and once the applicant/sponsor has provided all the necessary information to the department and has completed all the tasks required for a Texas Paddling Trail, the department will assist the local partner with a dedica-

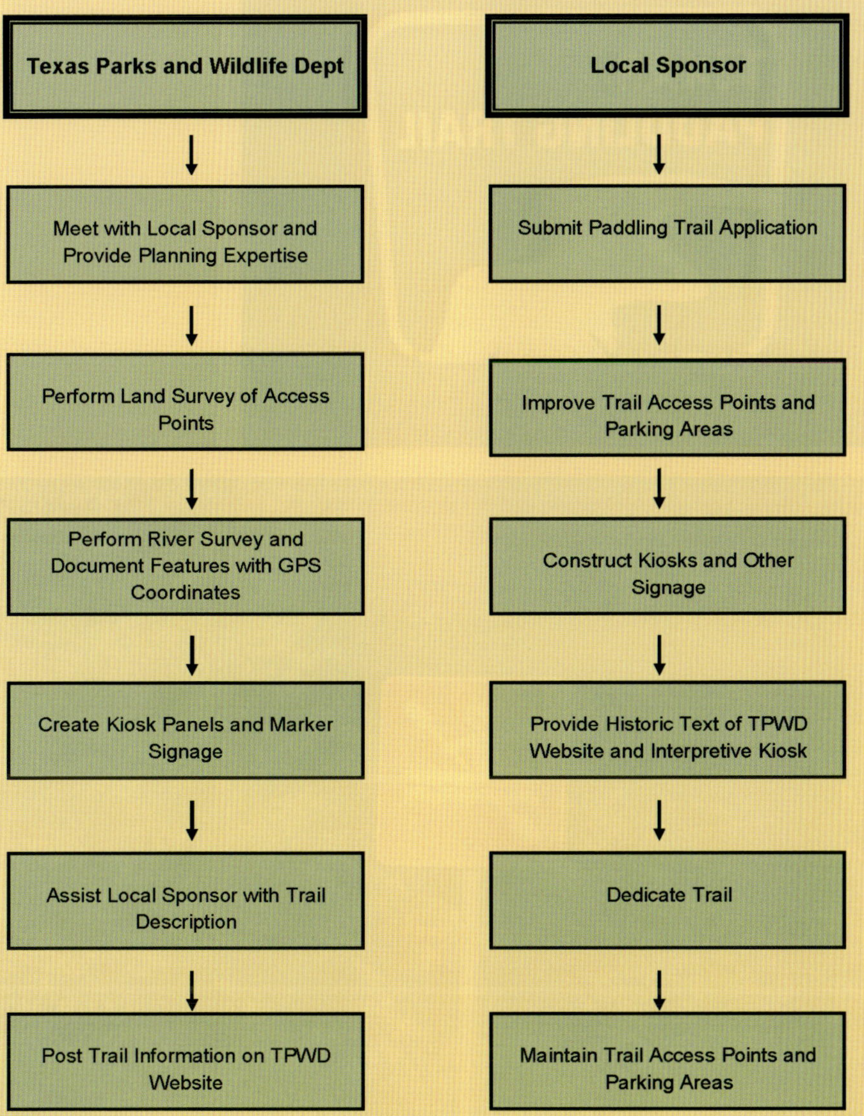


**FIGURE 7.4.** Shared responsibilities of TPWD and trail sponsor

**FIGURE 7.5.** Photographs of Paddling Trail signage

tion of the trail. Trail information is posted on the Texas Parks and Wildlife Department's paddling trails website (www.tpwd.texas.gov) and the trail becomes part of a statewide system of trails sanctioned by the department. Since the initiation of the paddling trails program, the acceptance of the program by local communities and the public has been overwhelming. Many communities have embraced the program as a way to bring ecotourism to their area. The city of Luling even painted a canoe with a paddler on their water tower to showcase the 6-mile-long Luling Zedler Mill Paddling Trail. The city also purchased some land along the river for a day-use park, enhanced access to the river, and improved the portage

**FIGURE 7.6.** Several paddling trail kiosks

**FIGURE 7.7.** City of Luling water tower

around Luling Dam. Other communities have also followed suit by hosting river fests, canoe races, and paddling tours to bring paddlers to their area. The paddling trails program has truly become a "win, win, partnership" between the state and local communities.

# 8 My Favorite Paddling Trails

I paddled my first state paddling trail in 1999, and over the past seventeen years I have been to all of the state's paddling trails. My wife, Joy, and I have traveled all over the state to paddle, and we shared river trips with our close friends, Brad and Colleen Belk (fig. 8.1). We have had some great adventures and witnessed wildlife that would not have been possible except from a canoe. Our dog, Hank, has been a constant companion over the past three years while we surveyed the state's paddling trails. He always wants to go along and doesn't want to be left behind. While riding in the canoe, he likes to sit in the bow and navigate the way (fig. 8.2).

**FIGURE 8.1.** Our paddling team (*left to right*) Colleen, Brad, Joy, and author with Olive and Hank in the foreground.
Courtesy of Brad Belk

The more than sixty trails offer a wide variety of habitats and waters to choose from, whether you enjoy the solitude of a quiet paddling experience on a lake, prefer going through a coastal marsh, want to test your skills on a whitewater stream in the Texas Hill Country, wind your way through a cypress swamp in East Texas, or paddle through an urban area surrounded by high-rise skyscrapers. If you want to camp somewhere with a paddling trail nearby, there are a number of trails that originate in state parks. Regardless of your preference, there is a paddling trail that will meet your expectations.

During my employment with the Texas Parks and Wildlife Department (TPWD), I was involved in the creation of a number of river trails and was also responsible for managing the coastal paddling trails. During the past three years, I revisited several of my favorites in an effort to compile information that may be helpful to you should you choose to visit them. I've included information on nearby trails that you may want to visit. I have also tried to describe the surrounding area and in some cases provided a little history. If you don't own your own boat, there are canoe and kayak liveries available that rent boats.

Information on liveries and more detailed information on all the trails are listed on the Texas Parks and Wildlife Department website at www.tpwd.texas.gov. Appendix 3 in this book also lists all the trails. I hope you will get out and paddle a trail of your choice. The experience will definitely be worth the effort.

**FIGURE 8.2.** Hank, our dog, navigates the way, while Joy and I paddle down the river

## INLAND TRAILS

With more than fifty inland trails to choose from—and the number continues to grow—it was difficult to narrow my selections for this book. I would recommend that you visit the TPWD website for more information on other trails. New trails are added each year so it's a good idea to revisit the website often. Because I have lived in Austin for many years and have paddled Lady Bird Lake on hundreds of occasions, I have included the Lady Bird Lake Paddling Trail here. I have also included several other inland trails you might want to try; they are located on Caddo Lake, B. A. Steinhagen Lake, the Guadalupe and South Llano Rivers, and Village Creek.

### Lady Bird Lake Paddling Trail

#### The Venue

The Colorado River meanders through downtown Austin in a west–east direction. In 1939 Tom Miller Dam was built on the river on the west side of town, and later in 1960, Longhorn Dam was constructed on the east side to form "Town Lake." In 2007, the 6-mile-long body of water was renamed Lady Bird Lake in honor of the former first lady, Claudia Alta Taylor Johnson, the wife of former president Lyndon Baines Johnson. Because the lake level is controlled by Tom Miller Dam, and water flowing into the lake occurs principally from low-flow hydropower turbines on the dam, current in the lake is minimal and, therefore, creates an ideal condition for rowboats and paddle craft. Powerboats with gasoline motors are prohibited, making the lake suitable for casual or hardcore paddlers who want to paddle upstream and downstream on quiet waters. Over the years, the lake and the shoreline have become a mecca of outdoor recreation for hiking, biking, and water-orientated sports. Each year the lake hosts sporting events such as triathlons, swimming competitions, canoe and kayak races, and rowing regattas. Rowing teams from colleges up north migrate south each year to train and enjoy the warm Austin temperatures, which are conducive to year-round paddling.

In 2009, the Texas Parks and Wildlife Department partnered with the Texas River School, Austin Parks and Recreation Department, and the Lower Colorado River Authority to create the Lady Bird Lake Paddling Trail. Three trails were created: Tom Miller Dam Loop (3.15 miles), Barton Springs Loop (3.25 miles), and the

Festival Beach Loop (4.8 miles) (fig. 8.3). On a busy summer day, I believe that the lake and paddling trails can attract more paddlers to this site than all other state paddling trails combined (fig. 8.4).

### TOM MILLER DAM LOOP TRAIL

There are two launch sites for the Tom Miller Dam Loop. (1) The Red Bud Road launch (30.291119 N, -97.787852 W) is located at 3401 Red Bud Trail on the west end of Lady Bird Lake. The launch is located on a small peninsula that jets out into the lake. The small parking lot holds only about twenty cars and fills up rapidly on weekends. (2) Another launch site is located at the Rowing Dock, a canoe/kayak livery on the south side of the lake at 2418 Stratford Drive (30.274523 N, -97.774210 W). This parking lot is small too and also fills up quickly, so arrive early. Otherwise, you can park on Stratford Drive. You can rent a boat at the Rowing Dock or launch your boat at a small dock near the livery.

### BARTON SPRINGS LOOP TRAIL

There are three launch sites for the Barton Springs Loop. (1) The first site is on the south side of the lake in Zilker Park at 2101 Andrew Zilker Road. There is a large parking lot in the park and Zilker Park Boat Rentals (30.2642824 N, -97.766788 W) is located south of the parking area on Barton Creek. (2) A second launch site is located on the north side of the lake at the Texas Rowing Center (30.272155 N, -97.768706 W) at 1541 Cesar Chavez Street. The Texas Rowing Center has rental canoes, kayaks, rowing sculls, and stand-up paddleboards or you can launch your own boat on the dock. The only parking at the site is along Cesar Chavez Street. (3) A third launch site is located on Cesar Chavez Street (30.270655 N, -97.765859 W) approximately 400 yards east of the Texas Rowing Center. There is a small parking lot on the south side of the road and a concrete-lined drainage ditch that leads down to the water. If you have your own boat, you can drive down to the water to launch.

### FESTIVAL BEACH LOOP TRAIL

The three launch sites from which to access the Festival Beach Loop are on the east end of the lake. (1) There is a boat ramp (30.248760 N, -97.728294 W) on the north side of the lake near the Holiday Inn. The Holiday Inn is located at 20 North IH 35. The boat ramp is on East Avenue, which runs along the lake shore. There are only six or eight parking spots near the ramp, yet there is some paid parking along the avenue. (2) There is a second launch site (30.251739 N, -97.735539 W) under the I-35 bridge on the north side of the lake that is only 75 yards east of

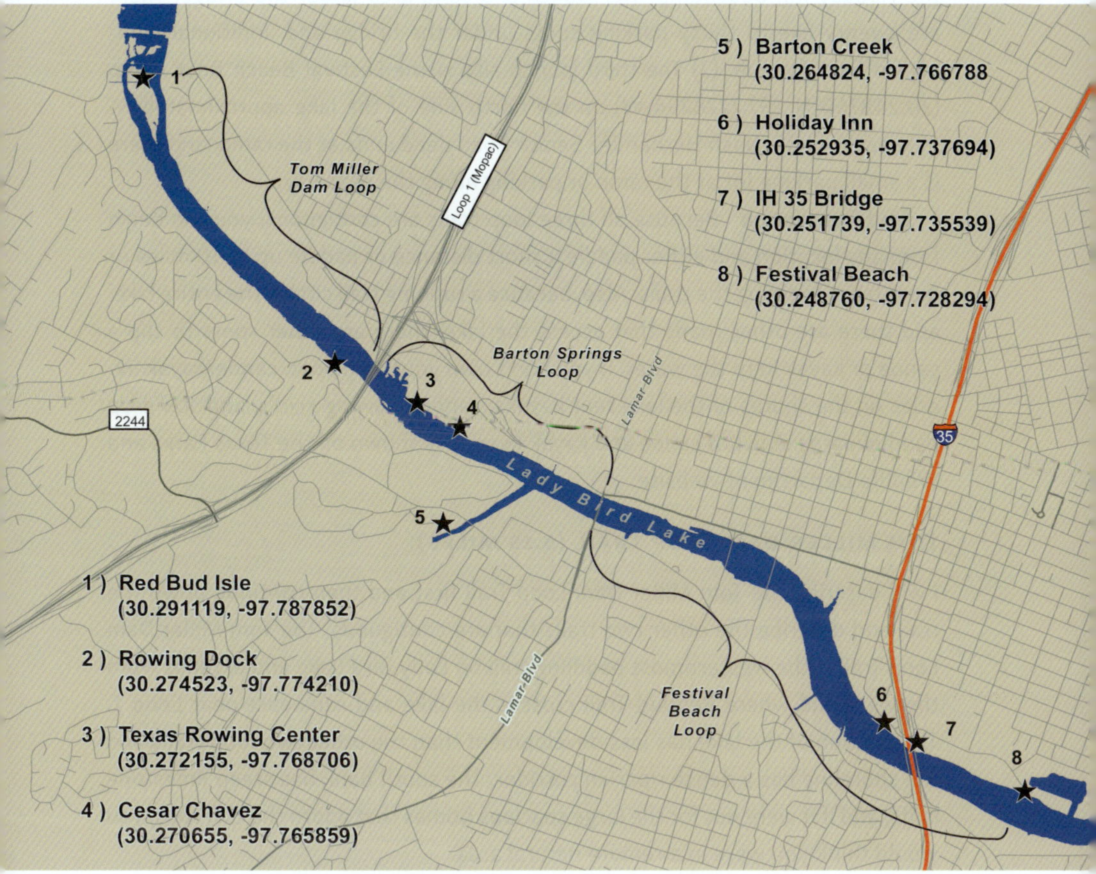


**FIGURE 8.3.** Lady Bird Lake Paddling Trails

**FIGURE 8.4.** Paddlers on Lady Bird Lake

the Holiday Inn boat ramp. The launch is a sand area under the bridge. There are twenty-five to thirty parking spots under the bridge and additional parking on East Avenue. (3) The third launch site is the Festival Beach Boat Ramp (30.248760 N, -97.7278294 W) on the north side of the lake approximately ½ mile east of I-35. Nash Hernandez Senior Road dead ends at the ramp, and there is a small parking lot at the ramp or parking along the roadway.

***Trail Description*** Because all three loop trails are contiguous, you can begin from any location and either paddle a short distance or paddle up to 10 miles or more by connecting the trails. Also, because a running trail circles the entire lake, and there are other roads that access the lake, there are other spots to slip a canoe or kayak in to the water. If you don't own your own boat, canoe/kayak liveries on the shores of the lake rent kayaks, canoes, rowing sculls, and stand-up paddleboards. A list of canoe and kayak liveries is shown on the Texas Parks and Wildlife Department website.

### TOM MILLER DAM LOOP TRAIL (3.15 MILES)

I will describe the Tom Miller Dam Loop Trail first and then continue down the trail and describe the other two trails that are contiguous. The Tom Miller Dam Loop Trail is the westernmost paddling trail on Lady Bird Lake and extends from the west end where Redbud Trail crosses the lake and runs east near Loop 1. This section of the lake has less development than the other two loop trails and the shoreline has a dense riparian corridor. The south bank has steep limestone cliffs, and if it were not for the large spacious homes that adorn the cliff tops, you would think you were in a remote natural area.

I normally launch at the Rowing Dock on south bank of the lake about 250 yards west of MoPac (Loop 1). If you own your own boat, there is a small public dock adjacent to the livery dock where you can launch. If you need to rent a canoe or kayak, the Rowing Dock is open in the morning and afternoon, so check the website for times (www.rowingdock.com).

If you choose to put-in there, you can paddle west toward Tom Miller Dam. Approximately 1 mile upstream from the put-in is an island that you will have to paddle around. You can paddle clockwise or counterclockwise around the island. If you choose to paddle counterclockwise around the right side of the island, you can see Tom Miller Dam straight ahead. If the water authority is generating power, you may see some turbulence below the dam. Don't worry, the flow is manageable, just keep your boat straight and you can easily paddle through the current. A few hundred yards before you reach the dam you will see a bridge where Redbud Trail crosses the lake. As you pass under the bridge, you will see another smaller island on your left. I once was attacked by a swan that had a nest on the island. I recall coming around the island and hearing a loud noise. Fifty yards to my left, a white swan was beating the water with its wings and trying to fly in my direction. I picked up the pace and the swan flew over to my boat and landed. There I was, almost eye to eye with the largest bird on the lake. I actually had to push the angry parent away from my canoe with my paddle to avoid being pecked. The swan was simply protecting its nest. Don't worry, I have not seen the swan nesting there since.

As you continue to paddle around the island, there are a few rocks in the main channel below the dam, but they are usually visible so you can avoid them. Next you will turn left and paddle across a small open water area. Up ahead there is a private road with a bridge you will have to pass under. Paddle under the bridge, turn left, and paddle under a second bridge where Redbud Trail crosses the water. As you paddle down a channel, the island is on your left and the south bank of the lake on your right. When you pass the island, you will be back in the main body of the lake, and up ahead on the right bank is the dock where you launched your boat. Once you reach the dock, you have completed the Tom Miller Dam Loop Paddling Trail. If you choose to paddle farther, the Barton Springs Loop Trail continues as you paddle east.

### BARTON SPRINGS LOOP TRAIL (3.25 MILES)

As you paddle east past the Rowing Dock, you will see more urban development as several major roads cross the lake; you can see the large office buildings of downtown Austin just north of the lake on your left. The waterfront is still quite scenic as the parks department maintains a running trail around the lake and there are many beautiful bald cypress trees that provide a lush riparian corridor. After passing under Loop 1 you will see a canoe and kayak livery on the north bank approximately 250 to 300 yards past the bridge. The livery is called the Texas Rowing Center. This is also a place where you can rent boats or launch your boat. After you pass the Texas Rowing Center, continue paddling east about 300 yards; you will see a concrete ramp on your left that leads down to the water. The ramp also carries rainfall down the drainage ramp and is a favorite canoe and kayak launch. There is limited parking near the ramp that is located on Cesar Chavez Drive, but street parking is also an option. Approximately 450 yards downstream of the concrete ramp on your right or south side of the lake, Barton Creek flows into the lake (fig. 8.5). As you turn right into the creek, you will see a gazebo to your right at Lou Neff Point. Paddling up the creek channel, you may see a healthy population of domestic ducks and geese.

**FIGURE 8.5.** Barton Creek

The water flowing out of Barton Creek channel is so clear that you can see several feet down into the water. There is a lot of submerged vegetation in the creek, and turtles are especially plentiful in warmer weather. If you paddle up the channel, approximately 400 yards ahead you will see a footbridge and then you will see a larger bridge where Barton Springs Road crosses over the channel. Farther up the channel you will see a number of canoes and kayaks sitting on the right bank. This is where Zilker Park Boat Rentals is located. After you paddle past the livery, the water will get shallow and will soon be too shallow to paddle—the bottom is hard rock. Just up ahead you will see a dam that impounds Barton Springs Swimming Pool. The pool covers approximately 3 acres and is known for its clear, cold (68–71 degrees) water. After you paddle you may want to take a swim in the pool.

Next, turn your boat around before the water gets too shallow and paddle back down the channel. When you reach the main body of Lady Bird Lake turn right to continue the Barton Springs Loop Trail. As you paddle east you will see Lamar Blvd. Bridge about 500 yards ahead. When you reach the bridge, you have reached the turnaround point.

### LONGHORN DAM LOOP TRAIL (4.8 MILES)

If you choose to paddle farther, the Lamar Bridge is the starting point for the Longhorn Dam Paddling Trail. After crossing under the Lamar Bridge, you will see two more bridges immediately ahead. The first is a large pedestrian bridge, and the second, a railroad bridge, is just beyond it. At the base of the support columns of the railroad bridge are a few trees where I have seen swans nesting in the past. As you continue, you will see the First Street Bridge about 800 yards up ahead. On the north side of the lake you will see the large downtown area. This area is quite scenic at night when all the towering buildings are lit up (fig. 8.6). On the south side of the lake is the running trail that follows the shoreline. On your right is an open area called Auditorium Shores where the city stages outdoor concerts and festivals. Approximately 300 yards before you reach the First Street Bridge on your right is a large 8-foot bronze statue of Stevie Ray Vaughn, an icon of blues guitar fame (fig. 8.7).

Once under the First Street Bridge, the Congress Avenue Bridge is approximately 300 yards ahead. Congress Avenue bisects the city's east and west sectors and the state capitol is straight north on Congress Avenue only thirteen blocks north of the lake.

As you continue to paddle east you will pass under the Congress Street Bridge. From March to November, you can witness a spectacular sight here. The bridge is the roosting site for a million and a half Mexican free-tailed bats that spend spring and summer in Austin (fig. 8.8). At dusk the bats stream out from the cracks under the bridge, forming a continuous cloud that flies into the night. Experts tell us that they eat from 20,000 to 30,000 pounds of insects each night.[1] Several canoe liveries have bat tours to watch the bats as they come out at dusk.

Approximately 350 yards past the Congress Bridge on the north (left) shore is the Waller Creek Boat House. The facility was complete in 2014 and has an array of paddling craft for rent. In addition to rowing shells, canoes, kayaks, and SUPs, the facility also has a café and fitness center. While the facility is quite

**FIGURE 8.6.** Nighttime view of downtown Austin from Lady Bird Lake Paddling Trail.
Courtesy of Texas Parks and Wildlife Department

**FIGURE 8.7.** Bronze statue of Stevie Ray Vaughn

## State Capitol Building

There is an interesting story about the state capitol building. It was built in 1888 of red Texas granite for a value of 3.7 million dollars. Instead of using money, the state traded 3,000,000 acres of land for the building. The land later became the XIT cattle ranch that stretched 200 miles across nine counties along the Texas–New Mexico border. The XIT cattle ranch became the largest privately owned cattle ranch in the world. Sadly, the ranch lasted less than thirty years and was sold off in smaller land parcels.

**FIGURE 8.8.** Mexican free-tailed bats.
Courtesy of Texas Parks and Wildlife Department

impressive, sadly there is no public parking, and patrons have to pay to park on the street. Just past the boat house, Waller Creek flows into the lake.

As you continue to paddle east, the lake makes a gentle bend to the right and then back to the left, and you can see the I-35 bridge up ahead. About 150 yards before you get to the bridge, a concrete boat ramp is on the north shore. The ramp is only one of two that I know of where motorboats can launch. Motorboats are allowed on the lake, but they can only use their trolling motors to navigate around. The one exception is the livery boats that are used to coach the rowing teams that train on the lake. Most fishermen who choose to fish on the lake, paddle kayaks or canoes.

After you pass under I-35, all the land on the north side of the road is park land, and a running trail runs right along the shoreline. The south bank is more developed, with several apartment complexes along the shore and an elevated hike and bike trail above the water that was completed in 2014.

Approximately ½ mile east of the I-35 on the north (left) shoreline is the other motorboat ramp with a small parking lot nearby. The ramp is on Festival Beach Road and is also a good place to launch a boat. At this point the trail ends, and if you turn around you can retrace your path to the launch site at the Rowing Dock. If you want to see the rest of the lake, you can continue to paddle east and approximately 300 yards ahead you will see a small channel on your left that leads into a lagoon at Festival Beach. The lagoon is approximately 400 yards long and is an excellent place to paddle when it is windy. If you continue to paddle past the lagoon, the lake will open up and you will see the small Snake Island up ahead. Once you pass the island and continue to paddle, you will see Longhorn Dam about ½ mile up ahead. This is the end of the lake.

***Wildlife*** Even though the lake is urban and there is an abundance of activity on most days, there is lots of wildlife as well. In particular, there is a large variety of bird species. Like most Texas waterways, there are great blue herons, but also snowy egrets, black-crowned night herons, green herons, American coots, pied-billed grebes, and several other water birds.

There are also a number of duck species. One of the most common is the wood duck; a resident population lives on the lake. In the spring, I occasionally see a female wood duck with her young. When I see them, I am reminded of the first time I saw a hen wood duck play the broken wing act. It was not on Lady Bird Lake but years ago in East Texas.

While paddling my canoe, I spotted a female with several young ducklings swimming in open water. As I approached the brood, the female wood duck immediately gave an alarm call and started flapping one wing and acting as if she were hurt and unable to fly. When I came closer, she swam away from her young and the ducklings ducked under water. After she had lured me quite a distance from her young, she stopped flapping her wing, sat up in the water, and then flew back in the direction of the ducklings. I was aware that she was only faking it, but I wanted to see the act.

In addition to wood ducks, there are several other species, including mottled ducks and an occasional mallard or bufflehead. Another common bird I see on the lake is the American coot, sometimes called "mud hen." In the winter, I often see large rafts of coots on the lake. They are small duck-like birds that are black with a white bill (fig. 8.9). The birds are not actually ducks, and instead of webbed feet

**FIGURE 8.9.** Coot.
Courtesy of Texas Parks and Wildlife Department

they have lobed feet that help them run across the water during takeoff. Because they are poor fliers, they have to get a running start to get airborne. If the wind is very strong, coots will run into the wind to get airborne, just like airplanes.

Cormorants are also frequent residents of the lake, and they too are terrible fliers. Cormorants are large black birds with hooked bills. While they don't fly well, they are great divers. They dive down into the lake to catch small fish.

You may also see a pair or two of white domestic swans on the lake. They look elegant as they swim along with arched necks. While I have seen young swans, called cygnets, over the years, I have also noticed that they disappear before they are fully grown. I suppose the local varmints are the culprit.

A number of species of turtles are found on the lake. Many are in the Barton Creek channel. Most of the larger ones are called sliders. Two of the most colorful are the red-eared turtles and Texas sliders. The red-eared turtle can be recognized by the red spot on the head just behind the ear (fig. 8.10), and the Texas slider has a beautiful yellow-colored pattern on the shell. I also have seen common snapping turtles in the water. Their large ornate shell, blunt head, and large claws distinguish them from other turtles. There are two species of snapping turtles: the common snapping turtle and the alligator snapping turtle. While both look almost prehistoric, the alligator snapping turtle (fig. 8.11) is a threatened species that gets much bigger than the common snapper and has large ornate spike-like projections on its shell and tail. Unlike other freshwater turtles, snapping turtles are seldom seen sunning along the banks. On rare occasions, I have also seen soft-shelled turtles in the lake.

**FIGURE 8.10.** Red-eared turtle with smaller soft shell turtle.
Courtesy of Texas Parks and Wildlife Department

**FIGURE 8.11.** Alligator snapping turtle

***Other Paddling Trails Nearby*** If you want to paddle another trail while in the area, several others trails are less than an hour's drive away. Fifty-six miles downstream of Longhorn Dam is the Wilbarger Paddling Trail. The trail launch is located at the FM 969 bridge crossing of the Colorado River (30.168287778 N, -97.40227778 W), a few miles outside the town of Bastrop. You can park under the 969 bridge or along the roadway shoulder, and there is a concrete boat launch. The trail is 14 miles long and has no major rapids, but there are a few rock gardens, and the river has several islands along the way. The trail ends in Bastrop at Fisherman's Park. The park has a boat ramp with a parking lot near the ramp. Fisherman's Park (30.11194444 N, -97.32497222 W) is also the launch site for the El Camino Paddling Trail, which extends downstream 6 miles to the Lost Pines Recreational Trails. The take-out is in a small park that has a dirt road that leads down to the water.

If you want to paddle another trail on a different river, the Luling Zedler Mill Paddling Trail is located near Luling about 45 miles from Austin. The launch site is located at Highway 90 (29.66790694 N, -97.69991083 W) and ends 6 miles downstream in the town of Luling at Zedler Mill. The take-out is on the right side of the river just before Zedler Dam. There is a small park on the right where you can drive down to the water and park.

## Village Creek Paddling Trail

### The Venue

The Village Creek Paddling Trail (fig. 8.12) is located in the eastern part of the state in a geographic area known as the "Big Thicket." While there are no specific boundaries for the Big Thicket, it roughly occupies several counties, including Liberty, Hardin, San Jacinto, Tyler, and Polk Counties. Described as one of the most diverse areas outside of the tropics, the Big Thicket has been recognized both nationally and internationally for its unique biological features.[2] On October 11, 1974, the US Congress passed legislation that authorized the Big Thicket National Preserve. The original legislation authorized an 84,550-acre area, which was only one of two national preserves managed by the National Park Service. Seven years later in 1981, the area was designated a Biosphere Reserve by the United Nations Educational, Scientific, and Cultural Organizations (UNESCO). Today, the Big Thicket National Preserve consists of 112,000 acres that include fifteen separate units and water corridors.

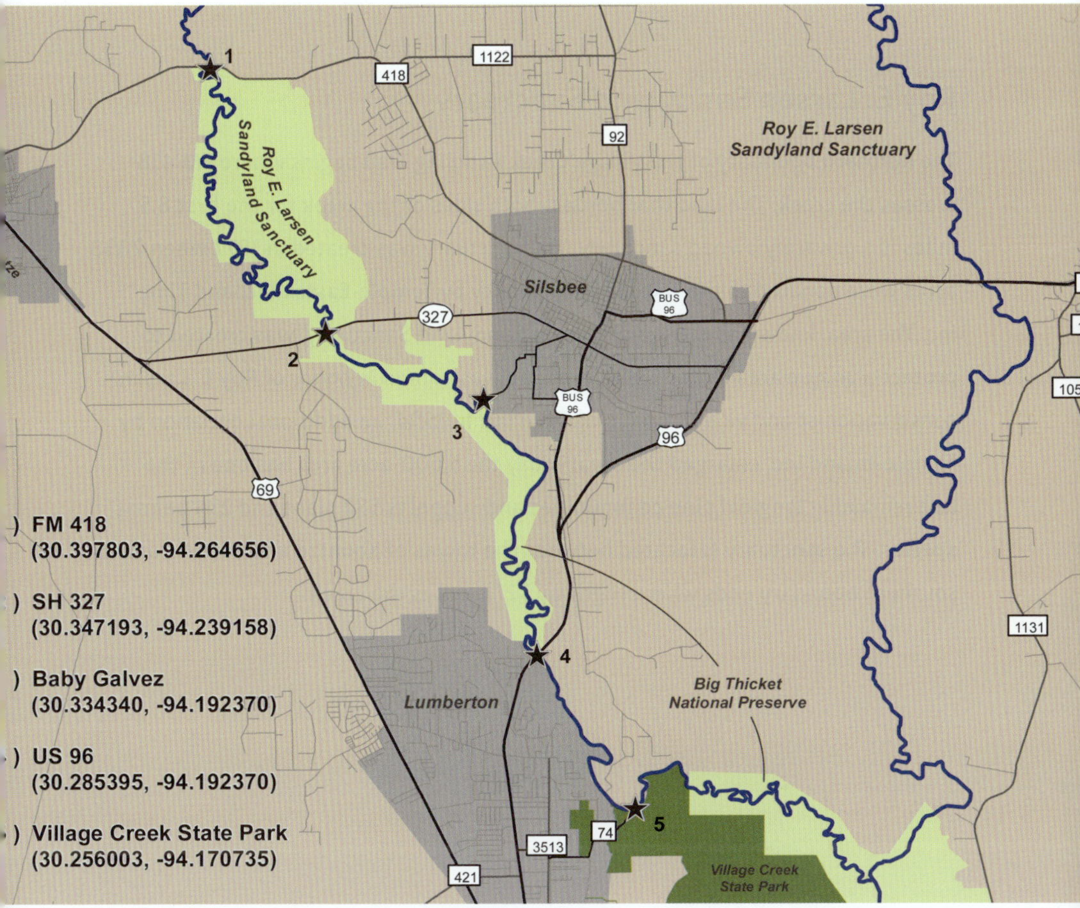


**FIGURE 8.12.** Village Creek Paddling Trail

***Put-in/Take-out*** Because the Village Creek Paddling Trail is 21 miles long, I would not recommend attempting to paddle the entire stretch in one day unless you are an extremely strong paddler or canoe racer who plans to paddle nonstop. However, there are multiple access points. You can paddle only a section of the trail, stay overnight, and paddle the remainder on the second day. Better yet, spend several days in the area, as the visit will be worth your time.

The trail begins at the FM 418 crossing of Village Creek (30.397803 N, -94.264656 W). From the town of Kountze, travel northeast on FM 418 for 3.2 miles to the creek. A large concrete bridge crosses the creek, and a dirt road leads down to the bridge. There is ample room to park near the bridge, and the

## Roy E. Larsen Sandyland Sanctuary

The northern boundary of the Village Creek Paddling Trail begins where FM 418 crosses the creek. The land that borders both sides of the creek for the first 8.5 miles is a privately owned sanctuary. The sanctuary was created in 1977 when 2,138 acres were donated to the Nature Conservancy by Temple-Eastex Inc. and Time Inc. The area, known as the Roy E. Larsen Sandyland Sanctuary, was created to protect a unique area of the Big Thicket and was named in honor of Roy E. Larsen, conservationist and vice chairman of Time Inc. In 1994, an additional donation by Temple-Inland Inc. enlarged the area. Today the 5,600-acre area has one of the last remaining longleaf pine communities and supports 582 plant and 234 animal species. The sanctuary is located between the towns of Kountze and Silsbee, and its southern boundary ends where Highway 327 crosses the creek.

road makes a U-turn under the bridge so you can pull back up to FM 418. Approximately 8 miles downstream from the 418 put-in is the SH 327 crossing. The put-in is near the large concrete bridge that crosses the creek, and there is parking near the bridge. If you choose to paddle the next section of the trail, continue to paddle another 2.9 miles to the Baby Galvez Road (30.334340 N, -94.192370 W). The Baby Galvez Road is located in the town of Silsbee. To get to the put-in, travel west from US 96 Bus on Lindsey Road and proceed west until it dead ends into Baby Galvez Road. Follow the Baby Galvez dirt road until it dead ends at the put-in. The next access point is located approximately 7.1 miles downstream at the US 96 (30.285395 N, -94.192370 W) bridge crossing. The last access point is in the Village Creek State Park (30.256003 N, -94.170735 W) approximately 3.2 miles downstream from US 96.

***Trail Description*** I last visited the trail in March 2016 with Joy and our intrepid neighbors, Brad and Colleen Belk. It is approximately 270 miles from my house in Austin, a five-hour drive. After loading our gear on February 28, we departed the following morning and arrived at Village Creek State Park around three in the afternoon. We wanted to take a good look around the area, so we decided to camp in the park. After spending the night in our campers, we all rose early to be on the river by ten.

We wanted to paddle the first two stretches of the trail, from the put-in at FM 418 to the take-out at Baby Galvez Road, approximately 11 miles downstream. After dropping a car at the Baby Galvez Road put-in, we drove to the FM 418 crossing of the creek on the north side of the Roy E. Larsen Sandyland Sanctuary.

The sandy soil in the sanctuary is a perfect setting for Village Creek, which meanders through the area. The stream has a sandy bottom with many white sand beaches scattered along the trail (fig. 8.13). We launched at about 10:30 a.m. and planned to paddle until we found a good sandy spot to have lunch.

As we pushed our canoes into the water, I was surprised at how dark it was. I knew that recent rains had washed silt into the stream, but the water was still a dark brown color. I suppose the tannin gave the water its chocolate hue. While many of the trees that line the banks were still sporting their winter coats, a few were beginning to sprout green leaves. I could only imagine how green and lush the trees would be once spring arrived.

Overhead, the clouds kept the sun at bay, but the sun was predicted to make an appearance around 1:00 p.m. Along the banks, here and there were beautiful yellow flowers growing on vines draped over the trees, forming the riparian corridor by the river. Up ahead I heard the familiar whistle of a wood duck just as a pair rose from the water and flew downstream.

**FIGURE 8.13.** Sandy beach on Village Creek Paddling Trail

As we paddled the first mile or so, the river curved right then left, and on every bend the sand stacked up, creating white beaches on the inside of the curve. Steep banks on the outside curve of the river were pitted and scarred by fast-moving water digging into the loose sand. Here and there, a downed pine tree was suspended over the water, undercut by higher flows. A few roots anchored the tree to the bank, keeping it from tumbling into the water. Its days were numbered until the next high flow swept it downstream. There were also downed trees in the water, but a quick steering stroke by my wife or an occasional draw in the bow kept our canoe clear of obstructions. As I looked around, I was disappointed to see ice chests, Styrofoam cups, and plastic bags littering the banks. Sadly, I see this far too often on Texas streams.

Ahead, a small bird flew downstream and perched on a tree overhanging the water. It was too dark to distinguish the bird's colors, but I recognized its flight pattern: a belted kingfisher.

At approximately mile 2, a metal bridge spans the river from bank to bank. The bridge is where the Timber Rock Railroad crosses the creek (fig. 8.14). While the Timber Rock Railroad is a small line, only 160 miles long, the parent company, Watco Transportation Company, is the largest privately owned short-line operator in the United States. With more than thirty-five railroads, and 4,500 miles of track, the company ships more than half a million carloads a year.

Just past the railroad bridge, a black vulture soared overhead and an American crow flew by, calling out as he passed. The river twists and turns and there are numerous sandy beaches throughout the first few miles of the trail. Somewhere around mile 5, I spotted one of my favorites, a great blue heron, up ahead. As we approached, he flew slowly downstream.

By noon, we'd covered 6 miles, so we pulled out on a sandbar to eat lunch. On a tree nearby we spotted yellow flowers growing on vines along the river. Upon closer inspection, we discovered they were Carolina jessamine (fig. 8.15). After a twenty-five-minute break, we launched our two aluminum canoes and paddled downstream. In the next few miles, the river starts to widen; bald cypress trees scatter along the banks. There is also an occasional magnolia tree and river birch growing along the water's edge. Tall long-leaf pine trees, growing back away from the water, towered over all the other trees. At mile 8, I saw the concrete bridge where SH 327 crosses the river. Just past the bridge, the river begins to widen and there are fewer curves. At approximately 10.1 miles from the put-in, there were two yellow and white pipeline markers on the left side near the creek.

**FIGURE 8.14.** Timber Rock Railroad Bridge crossing the trail at mile 2

**FIGURE 8.15.** Carolina jessamine vines draped on trees along trail

At mile 10.5, the river splits, and according to the screen on our GPS receiver, the two tributaries flow back together a short distance ahead. Instinctively, we chose to follow the flow and took the left channel. After paddling 0.3 miles, our channel rejoined the other; we had made the right choice. We caught sight of a bird perched in the top of a tree up ahead. From that distance, it was too hard to identify so we slowed our pace to try to sneak up on it. As we paddled under its tree, I recognized the red crest of a pileated woodpecker. With their dashing red topknot and striking black with white stripes, these woodpeckers are beautiful birds (fig. 8.16).

As we approached our take-out at Baby Galvez Road, there was a metal sign nailed to a tree on the right side of the river. The sign read Trash Can and an arrow pointed to the take-out on the left bank (fig. 8.17). We completed our trip, and my GPS said we paddled 10.9 miles. Before we'd finished pulling our canoes from the water, we had already made plans to return the next day and continue downstream.

March 2, 2016—After a good night's sleep, and pancakes and eggs for breakfast, we loaded our equipment into the car and dropped it off at the take-out. We were going to put-in at Baby Galvez Road and paddle to the take-out on the Neches River, 18 miles downstream. Even though the Village Creek Paddling Trail ends at the park, we wanted to see the confluence with the Neches River. We decided to paddle an extra 9 miles or so to the downstream take-out.

**FIGURE 8.16.** Pileated woodpecker

**FIGURE 8.17** Trash can sign at Baby Galvez Road take-out

A little after 10:00 a.m., we launched our canoes. My wife and I paddled our slightly worn Alumacraft aluminum canoe; our friends, Brad and Colleen, were also in an Alumacraft. Approximately 1 mile from the put-in, Brad paddled to the left bank and began surveying the area. I knew immediately that he was looking for, a geocache. What is a geocache? A geocache is a container, which often holds other objects, that has been hidden; its location has been posted on the Internet for others to find. It's like a worldwide hide-and-seek game. Anyway, it didn't take long for Brad to spot a small container hanging from a bald cypress limb. After taking a picture of the geocache, we paddled on downstream.

At approximately 1.4 miles from the launch, I spotted our first bird of the day, a belted kingfisher. As we paddled near, he took off toward a tree and perched on a branch that reached out over the creek. For the next mile or so, he continued to lead our canoe down the river. Bald cypress trees formed the riparian corridor, with a mixture of birch and elm trees. There is also an occasional magnolia tree and pine tree set back, away from the water. At mile 2.7 large power lines cross the river, and just beyond, the creek makes a sharp left turn. At mile 4 the river splits, and the map on our GPS receiver showed that we could take either fork since they converged a short distance downstream. We chose to go left since the flow was more pronounced in that channel. After we paddled less than ½ mile, the two channels came back together; again, we had made the right decision.

By 11:30 a.m., after paddling 4.8 miles, we pulled out on an inviting, sandy beach and stretched our legs. Oh, I forgot to mention that we brought along our two dogs, Hank and Olive, on this stretch. They both are great river dogs, and we have taken them on a number of paddling trails. Hank is a red miniature dachshund with short legs, floppy ears, and a chest that almost drags on the ground. Olive is a red miniature pinscher (Min Pin) with skinny legs and a chunky body. When out of the canoes, the dogs began to run and play, and Hank promptly began to dig in the soft sand (fig. 8.18). After a fifteen-minute break, we put back in and paddled downstream. At mile 5.6, we passed under the Highway 96 bridge. There were bank fishermen near the bridge and a motorboat launch on river left. We continued downstream, and this section of the river had more trees that were sporting their new leaves.

At mile 6.5, Timber Rock Railroad crosses the creek again. Several large buildings with green metal roofs line the right side of the river, and a gazebo graces the right bank. Since we were no longer in Big Thicket National Preserve, these were all private residences. For the next 1½ miles, there are

**FIGURE 8.18.** Hank having fun digging in the sand

**FIGURE 8.19.** Sandy beach where we stopped for lunch

numerous houses on the left bank and signs along the river reading, Village Creek Club. At mile 8.75, we could see the Village Creek State Park take-out on the right bank. There is a blue and white paddling trail sign on the bank and a sandy area to take-out. Because lunchtime was upon us, we pulled over on a sandy beach across from the park to enjoy our meal (fig. 8.19). Once again, the dogs ran up and down the white sand. Hank started digging in the soft white sand and disappeared in a hole.

After lunch, we paddled several miles until we came to an obstruction in the river. At mile 11.75, a large pine tree had fallen from the left bank, blocking the river. After scouting out the situation and seeing there was a good sand bank on the right, we portaged right and were able to get back into the river. At approximately 15.1 miles from the launch at Baby Galvez Road, Village Creek flows into the Neches River. In the river, the current picks up, but so does the headwind. At mile 17, we reached the Lakeview Sandbar take-out and pulled our canoes out of the river. Tired but happy we completed our trip at 2:45 p.m. What a great day on the river!

***Other Paddling Trails Nearby*** On March 3, before returning home, we paddled another nearby trail. The trail is called Cooks Lake to Scatterman Paddling Trail. It is approximately 6 miles north of Beaumont and located in the Beaumont Unit of the Big Thicket National Preserve. To get there from Beaumont, take Highway 69/96 north of IH 10 approximately 2 miles and exit on Lucas Drive. Proceed east on Lucas Drive approximately 1 mile and turn left, then head north on Bigner Road. There is a large white sign at the entrance of the Lower Neches Valley Authority (LNVA) property. Follow the road until it dead ends at the LNVA facility. There is a large parking lot and a concrete motorboat ramp at the put-in. A saltwater barrier (dam) near the put-in prevents saltwater from intruding upstream during dry periods when river flows are low (fig. 8.20). Although the trail is less than 5 miles long, a portion of the trail meanders through a heavily wooded bald cypress/tupelo swamp, a unique feature.

**FIGURE 8.20.** Saltwater barrier/dam on the Neches River at the Cook's Lake to Scatterman Paddling Trail put-in

After we left the put-in, we paddled up the Neches River and bore left at the first fork into Pine Island Bayou. We continued to paddle up the bayou and kept right when the channel forked. We were then in Cook's Lake. Approximately 1.4 miles from the put-in, Cook's Lake begins to narrow. We followed the channel for ½ mile until the channel was blocked by bald cypress and tupelo trees. This is where the trail ends, so we turned around.

Over near the bank I spotted a large white flower. Upon closer inspection, there were many green plants growing in the shallow water, but only one beautiful white cluster of petals. The long delicate petals that drooped downward seemed fragile for this otherwise harsh environment. However, the flower derives its name from the area; it was a swamp lily (fig. 8.21). Swamp lilies are native to the area and grow throughout the Big Thicket.

**FIGURE 8.21.** A solitary swamp lily in Cook's Lake

After the turnaround, we retraced our path back toward the put-in for a short distance. We kept left into a small channel that meandered through a dense woody bald cypress/tupelo swamp. The path would be impossible to follow if it were not for the National Park Service stakes and red flagging tied to limbs that lead the way (fig. 8.22). As we paddled along, I marveled at the beautiful, massive trees and thought about what it must have been like for early pioneers who had no map or trail to follow (fig. 8.23). It would be easy to get turned around in this maze. As we exited the thick cover of trees, a dark brown bird soared through the trees and disappeared. While I only caught a quick glimpse, I am sure it was an anhinga. The anhinga is a water bird often mistaken for a cormorant. They are dark colored and dive for fish, just like cormorants. However, the anhinga has a sharp bill, whereas the cormorant has a hooked bill. I think this is the first I have seen on a paddling trail.

After leaving the swamp, we paddled across the lake and bore right. At approximately 3.1 miles from the put-in, the water opens up, and we were back in the Neches River. We followed the river and returned in less than two hours.

**FIGURE 8.22.** National Parks Service signs marking the paddling trail through the cypress tupelo swamp

**FIGURE 8.23.** A bald cypress tree in the cypress tupelo swamp

## Martin Dies Jr. State Park Paddling Trails

### The Venue

The Big Thicket is a region spanning five counties in East Texas. Nationally recognized as one of the most diverse habitats in the country, the area with its large cypress trees, hardwood forest, and black water swamp provides habitat for a wide variety of wildlife. At least three hundred kinds of birds; eighty-six reptile and amphibian species; 1,320 trees, vines, grasses, and flowering plants; sixty mammals; ninety-seven species of fish; and four kinds of carnivorous plants are found there.[3] Unlike other plants, carnivorous plants derive their nutrients not from the soil or water; they ingest insects and arthropods that are attracted and trapped by the plant.[4]

On the northern edge of the Big Thicket are four paddling trails. I have paddled all four, but my two favorites are the Walnut Slough and Neches Paddling Trails (fig. 8.24). Both are located on Lake B. A. Steinhagen. The lake was impounded in 1953 for recreation and power generation and today has become a popular destination for all types of recreation. This 10,687-acre lake, also known as "Dam B," straddles the Tyler and Jasper County lines. With its irregular shape, serpentine channels that intersect with the Neches River, and beautiful cypress trees, the lake provides a scenic setting for a short paddle or several days on the water.

Land access is by way of Martin Dies Jr. State Park. The 730-acre park, named for attorney, judge, state representative, and US congressman Martin Dies Jr., is made up of three land parcels that border the lake. The park is located on Highway 190 approximately 12 miles west of Jasper and 17 miles east of Woodville; it has primitive campsites, cabins, screened shelters, and RV hookups. There are several lighted piers in the park that provide catfish, bass, perch, and crappie fishing spots for the skilled angler. The park has a swimming area in the Hen House Ridge Unit, and several miles of hiking and biking trails cut through the trees. The diverse forested habitat in the park, interspersed with the sloughs and lake habitat, provide an abundance of wildlife and birding opportunities for park visitors.

I last visited the park in April 2014, along with my wife, Joy, and neighbors Brad and Colleen. We pulled our campers to the site and spent the night in the Hen House Ridge Unit of the park on the south side of Highway 190. Joy and I brought our 17-foot Alumacraft aluminum canoe; Brad and Colleen also had their Alumacraft. Brad, who likes to paddle solo occasionally, brought along his Wenonah Kevlar voyager solo canoe. Since our campsite was near the water, we only

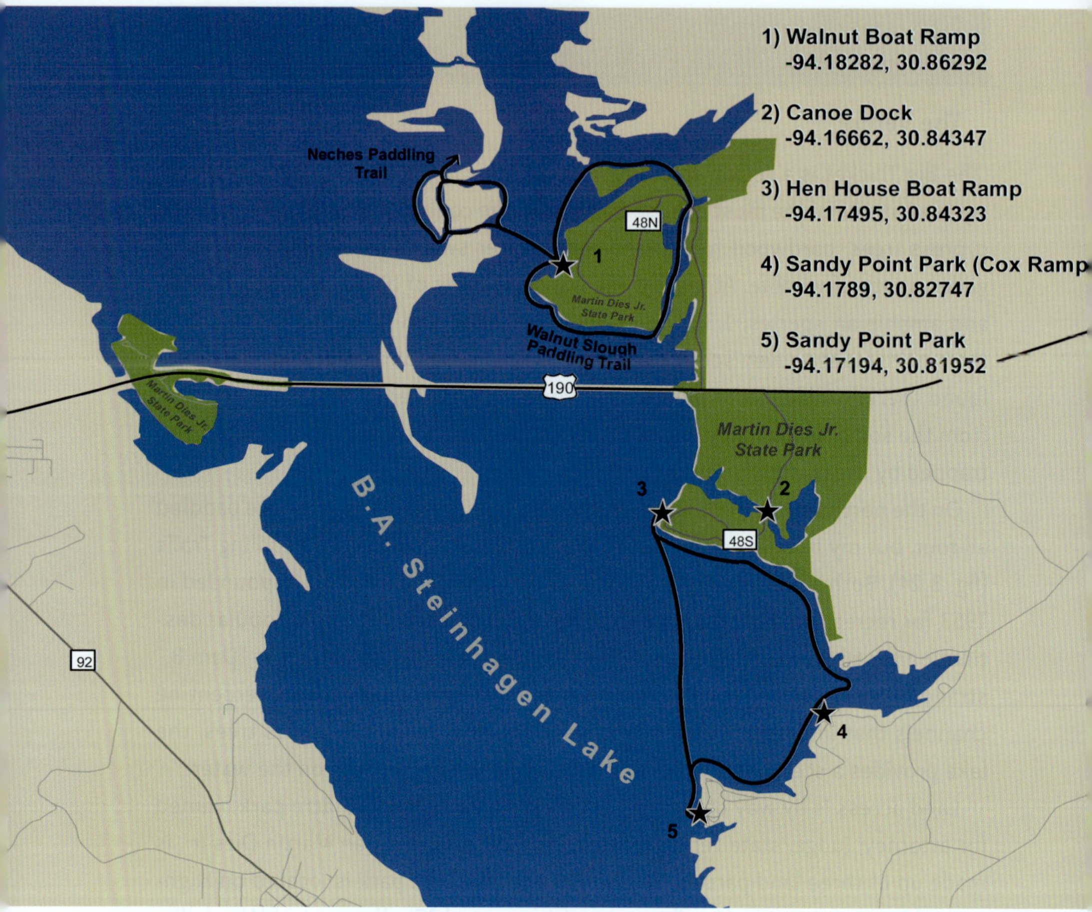


FIGURE 8.24. Martin Dies Jr. State Park Paddling Trails

had to carry our canoe a short distance to launch. I had been to the park in the past, but was excited because this would be my first chance to paddle the trails.

***Put-in/Take-out*** There are actually three trails to choose from in the park. The Walnut Slough Paddling Trail (4.3 miles) and the Neches Paddling Trail (3.2 miles or longer) are located north of Highway 190 and can be accessed from the Walnut Ridge Unit of the park. The Sandy Creek Paddling Trail (4.9 miles) is located in a portion of the lake south of the Hen House Ridge Unit of the park. There are also five boat ramps/docks in the park that are listed below that can be used to access the lake and paddling trails. Four of the access points are south of Highway 190 and provide access to the Sandy Creek Paddling Trail, while the Walnut Boat Ramp is the only ramp located on the Walnut Ridge Unit, north of

Highway 190. This is the best place to access the Walnut Slough and Neches Paddling Trails.

The names and the GPS coordinates of the five access points are listed below:

Walnut Boat Ramp—30.86292 N, -94.18282 W
Canoe Dock—30.84347 N, -94.16662 W
Hen House Boat Ramp—30.84323 N, -94.17495 W
Sandy Point Park (Cox Ramp)—30.82747 N, -94.1789 W
Sandy Point Park—30.81952, -94.17194 W

***Trail Description*** On April 21, 2014, my wife and I arrived at the park around ten thirty in the morning. After lunch, Joy and I loaded Hank, our dog, in our canoe and Brad loaded Olive, his dog, in his solo boat, and we launched our canoes from the shoreline near our campsite. Since the weather was nice, we paddled from our campsite on the Hen House Ridge Unit to the Walnut Slough Paddling Trail. If you camp or drive to the Walnut Ridge Unit you can put-in at the Walnut boat ramp.

After we left our campsite, we paddled under Highway 190 to reach the Walnut Slough Trail. The trail is a loop course that circles the western portion of the Walnut Ridge Unit. We chose to paddle the trail in a counterclockwise direction, so we headed north through Walnut Slough, which bisects the unit. The slough is a beautiful area lined with cypress trees. Ahead we saw several wood storks sunning in a tree near the channel (fig. 8.25). When we reached the northern end of the slough, we paddled under a small bridge where Park Road 48 crosses the water. Turning left, we continued on as the water opened up into the main body of the lake; ahead was a small island. We kept right around the smaller island and followed the shoreline of the larger Walnut Ridge Unit. After paddling a short distance, we intersected the Neches Paddling Trail. We eventually returned to the mouth of Walnut Slough and followed the shoreline, paddling south, then east, and then completed the 4-mile trail in about two hours.

Back at camp, Joy and I, with our dog Hank in tow, checked out the Neches Paddling Trail. We retraced our path to the Walnut Ridge Unit, but paddled clockwise around the island until we reached the point where the Neches Paddling Trail begins. We paddled north-northeast and followed a channel that wound its way toward the river. There was a thick mat of water hyacinth covering the water and ahead several snowy egrets (fig. 8.26) standing in the hyacinth. When Hank, our dog, saw the birds, he jumped out of the boat and plunged into the water. Apparently, he thought the dense mat of vegetation was solid. Luckily, I grabbed his leash and pulled him back into the boat—that was a close one.

**FIGURE 8.25.** Wood storks sunning in a tree near the Walnut Slough Paddling Trail

**FIGURE 8.26.** Snowy egret.
Courtesy of Texas Parks and Wildlife Department

This portion of the lake has a number of alluvial islands that were created by the junction of the Neches and Angelina Rivers. Fortunately, there are several buoys that mark the trail. However, we must have missed one because our channel came to an end. We turned around and retraced our path. We knew that if we continued to circle around the island that we would enter another channel. Just beyond this island is the river. Sure enough, we entered the channel headed north to the Neches River. Once in the river, we turned left and let the flow take us south.

After paddling downstream for 500 yards, we came across a buoy marking the trail, and we turned left. To return to the park, we paddled around the two islands and rejoined the trail that led back to it.

With the Walnut boat ramp just ahead, we spied a floating log in the channel. Instinctively my wife made several draw strokes to avoid a collision. As we passed the log, we notice it had eyes. Oh, my gosh—it was an alligator! Immediately I grabbed Hank, who was perched on the bow of the canoe. Fortunately, he never saw the gator. Hank has a bulldog attitude and a dachshund body, which sometimes gets him in trouble!

***Wildlife*** Over the past seventeen years, I have been to all the trails and paddled hundreds of miles. In doing so, I have seen some beautiful areas and viewed wildlife that would not have been possible except by canoe. My trip to B. A. Steinhagen Lake was no different. While paddling the trail, I saw a number of water birds, including great blue herons, great egrets, little blue herons, cormorants, snowy egrets, and some others. I also saw common grackles, red-winged blackbirds, a cardinal, and a red-headed woodpecker.

While paddling on the Neches Paddling Trail, I also saw a bird that I had not seen on any other trail. On April 2, 2014, my wife and I saw several birds in the thick floating vegetation. As we paddled closer, we recognized, to our delight, a common gallinule. Common gallinules, sometimes called swamp hens, are rails and are taxonomically in the Rallidae family. With its gray back, long spindly legs, and rich red frontal shield that extends up between its eyes, the bird is rather odd looking (fig. 8.27). Common gallinules have long yellow legs and distinctly long, spindly toes that spread the bird's weight over a larger area when they walk. With this special adaptation, the bird can walk on floating water lilies, yellow lotus, or other floating vegetation. It can walk on water, almost! As mentioned earlier, alligators are frequently seen in the lake and the adjoining Neches River.

Since my visit to the park, I learned from Charles Hubbard, assistant park manager, that the trails have now been marked with white PVC pipes that are

**FIGURE 8.27.** A common gallinule walking across water hyacinth near the Neches Paddling Trail

color coded and have TPWD written in black paint on the pipes. This should prevent you from getting lost, as my wife and I did.

***Other Paddling Trails Nearby*** Immediately adjacent to the Neches Paddling Trail is the Beliport Paddling Trail. On my last trip to the park, we paddled the trail. It is straight north of the park approximately 4 miles, as the crow flies. The put-in is on FM 2799 (30.92396667 N, -94.16690833 W). The first several miles of the trail follow the Angelina River. At approximately 5.5 miles from the put-in, the Angelina flows into the Neches River. During my last visit, we saw three alligators near the junction of the two rivers. After you enter the Neches, follow it approximately 3.1 miles until you see a buoy on the left side of the river that marks the Neches Paddling Trail. If you turn left (east) at the buoy, you will be back on the Neches trail. The distance from the put-in to the Walnut boat ramp in the park is approximately 9.3 miles.

## Upper Guadalupe–Nichol's Landing Paddling Trail

### The Venue

The headwaters of the Guadalupe River originate in Kerr County in an area known as the Texas Hill Country. From its origin in the county, the river flows in a southeast direction, emptying into San Antonio Bay on the Texas coast. The river is roughly 230 miles long and drains 6,070 square miles. By Texas standards, the river is not large, and in fact, the basin is only the tenth largest river basin, but it is still larger than four states: Rhode Island, Delaware, Connecticut, and Hawaii. Truly, everything is bigger in Texas.

The upper reaches of the river are characterized by sheer banks, limestone cliffs, and beautiful bald cypress trees that line the stream. The terrain is subject to fast-moving water and flooding during times of heavy rainfall. Some sections of the Guadalupe have rock gardens, rock ledges, and rapids, which are sought after by whitewater enthusiasts. The stream is also a popular choice for canoeists, kayakers, and tubers, especially in the spring and summer (fig. 8.28). Due to an ever-increasing use of the river for all types of water recreation, and in order to protect the habitat, the Texas legislature passed legislation creating the Water Orientated Recreation District (WORD) in 1987. The purpose of WORD was to improve the environmental condition of the river by conserving natural resources, improving public health, and promoting water safety.

The geographic boundary of the district includes Canyon Reservoir and 30 miles of stream above or below the dam in Comal County. This section of the river is the most heavily used. To achieve its mandated task, WORD issues permits to water-based businesses and collects user fees. The fees are used to provide law enforcement along the river, support river cleanups, and promote responsible water use as well as safe water recreation through education and outreach programs.

I recall taking a float trip with a group of friends on a warm summer day in the early 1990s. I distinctly remember the number of tubers on the river downstream of Canyon Lake. It was a warm summer day, the water was cool and refreshing, and I was glad to be there. After floating down the river for half an hour, we came across two men standing in the water up ahead. They looked out of place, as they were not wearing swim trunks, but instead official-looking uniform shirts and shorts. They appeared to be inspecting the ice chest of some of the tubers, and as we approached, the officials looked our way, greeted us, and asked to look inside our ice chests. I realized that the two must be checking for glass containers or Styrofoam, which are both prohibited in the district. Fortunately, we were aware of the regulation and happily opened our ice chest to let them look inside. The officials politely wished us well, and we floated on down the river.

***Put-in/Take-out*** There are three points of access to the 9.9-mile Upper Guadalupe–Nichol's Landing Paddling Trail (fig. 8.29). The upper put-in is located at Nichol's Landing on Spring Branch Road (29.879416 N, -98.448278 W). The put-in has a nice paved area to use to pull down to the river and unload your canoes, and there is also ample parking along the entry road. The parking is free except on weekends or major holidays from Memorial Day to Labor Day. Approximately 5.4 miles downstream from the put-in is an alternate access point at the FM 311 road crossing (29.860670 N, -98.383771 W). There is a small gravel parking area

**FIGURE 8.28.** The Guadalupe is a beautiful river that is popular for all types of recreation. Courtesy of Texas Parks and Wildlife Department

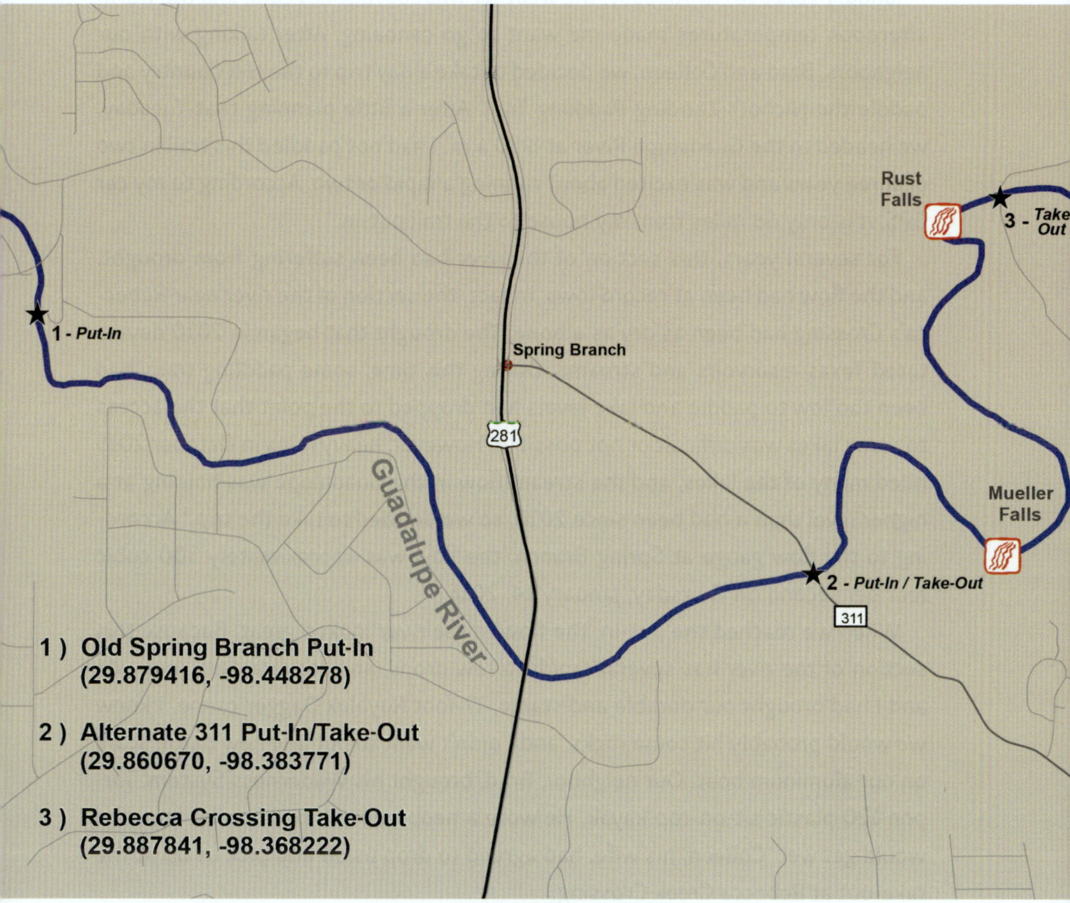


**FIGURE 8.29.** Upper Guadalupe / Nichol's Landing Paddling Trail

on the northeast side of the FM 311 bridge, but you will have to carry your boat down a concrete embankment approximately 100 yards to the river. The downstream take-out is located at Rebecca Creek Crossing (29.887841 N, -98.368222 W), and there is a paved road that leads down to the water. If you need to rent a boat or need a shuttle, several liveries are listed on the Texas Parks and Wildlife Department website, www.tpwd.texas.gov.

***Trail Description*** I feel fortunate to live in Texas where the winters are mild compared to the winters up north. In fact, except for a few cold fronts, the average temperature is above 60 degrees during the winter months in Austin. My friends who live in the New England area are not so lucky. Many of the rivers are frozen over, and paddlers can't canoe until April.

January 12, 2016—a Tuesday, the weather was cool but not cold, and the warm afternoon temperatures made me want to go canoeing. After talking with our neighbors, Brad and Colleen, we decided to take a day trip to the Hill Country and paddle the Nichol's Landing Paddling Trail. After a little planning that Tuesday, we headed to the Guadalupe River at 8:30 a.m. I had not paddled this trail in two or three years and was excited about running a rapid or two. According to my car GPS, it is only 68 miles from my house to the trail put-in.

For several years, this section of the river had been suffering from drought, and the flow had been at record lows. In fact, the section of the river near Rebecca's Crossing had been as dry as a bone. The drought that began in 2010 devastated Texas reservoirs and streams. During this time, some paddling trails had been too low to paddle and lake levels had dropped to the point that the access to some lakes was difficult or not possible. However, heavy rains in October 2015 filled many of the lakes, and the stream flow in the Guadalupe was holding at a higher level than it had been since 2010, so we decided to take the trip.[5] According to the flow gauge at Spring Branch, the flow was approximately 300 cubic feet per second on Thursday, January 14, 2016.

When we reached the put-in, the flow in the river looked great. Because this section of the river has several rapids, a few drops, and rock gardens, my wife and I had brought our durable and stable, 17-foot Royalex Dagger canoe. I knew we would probably hit some rocks, and I didn't want to put any new battle scars on our aluminum boat. Our neighbor, Brad, brought his Wilderness System, Tarpon 120 plastic sit-on-top kayak. He wore a neoprene suit because he knew he would get wet. Colleen, his wife, had agreed to drop us off and pick us up at the take-out at Rebecca Creek Crossing.

We put-in at the Old Spring Branch Road. Several stepping stones on the bank allowed me to get in the canoe without wetting my feet—at least for the moment. While I normally paddle the bow, and my wife paddles the stern, we switched positions that day. This gave us both a chance to test our skills because this stream has more rocks, drops, and whitewater than most of the other paddling trails. By changing positions, we created one slight problem with our trim. Most tandem canoes are designed to have the heavier paddler in the bow and the lighter person in the stern. Because I weigh about 50 pounds more than Joy, the stern would sit lower in the water than the bow. This would cause the canoe to drag the bottom when we paddled through shallow areas. I needed to keep the canoe pointed in the same direction as the current when we paddled over rocks and through the shallows or we would be forced to take a swim.

Approximately 0.75 miles from the put-in, we paddled through a shallow riffle area and bumped a rock or two, but we made it through without incident. Just up ahead I saw our first great blue heron (fig. 8.30). This is one of the most common birds to see on Texas rivers. Large bald cypress trees, scattered along the banks, are also characteristic of Hill Country streams. These trees not only provide a place of refuge for many birds and small mammals, but the root system also forms a massive barrier along the shore that holds the soil and prevents erosion.

At approximately 3 miles from the launch, a rocky shelf dropped quickly, and my wife had to draw the bow right and left with cross bow corrective strokes to avoid rocks. As we neared the Highway 281 bridge, the river deepened and became lake-like. Immediately past Highway 281, the water got shallow, and we got hung up on a rock. The current spun our canoe around and we instinctively leaned downstream. At first, we tried to push off the rock with our paddles, but when that failed, I stepped out and pushed our canoe free.

**FIGURE 8.30.** A great blue heron resting on one foot. Courtesy of Texas Parks and Wildlife Department

Approximately ½ mile past the Highway 281 bridge, we heard the familiar sound of water rushing against rocks, which meant a rapid was up ahead. As we drew nearer, we could not see beyond where the river dropped over a rocky ledge and bald cypress trees grew in the channel. It was difficult to determine the best pathway through the rapid. We instinctively stayed in the middle of the river; we would decide at the last second to go left or right, as needed. Luckily, we dropped over the small rocky ledge, skimmed over a few rocks, and made it through the rapid without taking on any water.

Approximately another ½ mile farther downstream, we heard the rushing sound of water once again; another rapid was up ahead. Again, cypress trees on islands in the stream blocked our view. We pulled over to scout the rapid. There were several rock ledges that would surely swamp our canoe and Brad's kayak, and we couldn't see a safe route downstream. There was a small channel running around the right side of the island and we could see water flowing back into the main channel about 100 yards downstream. Because the channel disappeared behind the island, we weren't able to see whether it was clear of obstructions. After some discussion, Brad opted to run the blind channel in his kayak. Once in the waterway, he disappeared behind the island; after a few anxious moments of us watching, he popped out downstream, still upright. He gave us the "thumbs up." Since he made it, we decided to give it a try too. Without hesitation, we paddled to the right bank, launched our boat over a small ledge, and followed the fast-moving water into the channel. Once in, the fast-moving water pushed our canoe against the banks, but after a few cross-bow draws and stern rudders, we made it through. What a great ride!

Up ahead a short distance, we stopped at the FM 311 bridge. After a short lunch break, we launched our boats with 4.5 miles to go before reaching the take-out. We knew that there were two falls waiting ahead that we may have to portage: Mueller and Rust Falls. After paddling approximately 1.6 miles downstream from FM 311, we saw Mueller Falls. There are cypress trees growing on an island in the stream, so we paddled up to the island, got out, and scouted the falls. The last time we paddled this trail, there was a narrow chute that flowed on the left side of the island. Upon further inspection, the chute seemed clear of obstructions, so Brad paddled over and dropped into the chute. After we made sure he reached the bottom of the falls, we launched our canoe and paddled to the chute. Once in, we needed to make a few steering strokes to avoid a tree root, but ultimately made it safely.

About ½ mile past Mueller Falls, we ran one small rapid, and ¾ of a mile past that, we paddled into a shallow area where we were forced to get out of our boats and walk them to deeper water. The last obstacle up ahead, the most difficult, was Rust Falls.

Rust Falls is less than ½ mile from the take-out and approximately 9.5 miles from the put-in at Spring Branch Road. As you approach Rust Falls, it is difficult to see which way to go because the river bends sharply to the left. In order to get a better look, we paddled safely over to the right bank to take-out. Standing on the bank, we saw that the river dropped several feet over the falls and there was no clear path on the right. However, a winding channel on the opposite side of the river looked runnable. After we had a short discussion, Joy reluctantly agreed to paddle over to the left side and take a better look. Brad, not sure which way to go, chose to stay on the right bank. Once in the channel, the fast-moving water took control of our canoe and volleyed us from side to side like a cork floating on water. The rushing water forced Joy to make several corrective strokes from the bow to prevent our canoe from turning broadside (fig. 8.31). When we were safely at the bottom of the falls, we congratulated each other on our success. We actually made it through in a dry boat! After completing the run, we paddled over to the right bank where Brad was still standing above the falls. To our surprise, he sat down in his kayak and pushed off the ledge. As his kayak plunged into the water, he capsized. Wet but unhurt, he climbed back into his kayak, and we all paddled the last ½ mile to the take-out without incident. What a great day on the river!

***Safety*** Because the Nichol's Crossing Trail is technically more difficult than many of the paddling trails, you should always take every precaution. Wear your life jacket at all times and scout every rapid and difficult-looking spot. If you are a novice, don't paddle the trail alone. If you paddle a tandem boat, put the more experienced paddler in the stern. When possible, paddle with other boats and let the most experienced boat take the lead. The two falls I mentioned earlier are

**FIGURE 8.31.** Bob and Joy successfully running Rust Falls.
Courtesy of Brad Belk

at least a class III, and unless you are experienced, I would not try to run them. Regarding the rapids and falls, remember, "When in doubt, get out and scout." Also, don't forget, this trail is regulated by WORD, and glass containers, Styrofoam, and small plastic containers are prohibited.

***Other Paddling Trails Nearby*** If you want to paddle another paddling trail, there are several to choose from. Approximately 45 miles due south of the Nichol's Crossing Paddling Trail is the Saspamco Paddling Trail. The trail is on Loop 1604 just southeast of San Antonio in Wilson County. This 12.1-mile section of the San Antonio River has no man-made obstructions, but like all streams, watch for snags and submerged logs when water levels are low. The trail is named after Saspamco, a small town nearby, and is an acronym for San Antonio Sewer Pipe Manufacturing Company. In 1901 the company began using red clay, found in the area, to manufacture clay pipe. By the 1930s, 150 people (75 percent of the residents) worked at the Saspamco plant. By 1960 the demand for clay sewer pipe declined as steel and poly vinyl chlorine pipe replaced it. Today approximately 450 people reside in Saspamco, Texas.

There are also two other paddling trails in the Seguin area that you may want to try. Both trails can be accessed from the Max Starcke Park. The Seguin Paddling Trail (Lake Seguin) is a 4-mile paddling trail that begins at the put-in near Saffold Dam and runs 2 miles upstream to the Highway 46 turnaround and then back to the put-in. The Seguin Paddling Trail (Lake Nolte/Meadow Lake) begins at the natural fishing area in Max Starcke Park and goes 5.8 miles downstream to Nolte Dam. There is an alternate put-in/take-out approximately 2.6 miles downstream of the park put-in. Depending on the distance you choose to paddle, you can vary your trip from 2.6 to as much as 11.6 miles.

## South Llano Paddling Trail

### The Venue

The South Llano Paddling Trail (fig. 8.32) is located in Kimble County near Junction, Texas. Take Interstate 10 to Junction and go south on US 377 for 5 miles. Turn on Park Road 73, which leads into the South Llano River State Park. After you enter the park, the put-in for the trail is at the Park Road 73 bridge that crosses the South Llano River.

The paddling trail begins in the South Llano River State Park, a major attraction in the county, and ends near Junction. The 2,650-acre parcel of land was donated to the state in 1977 by Walter Buck. The spring-fed South Llano River

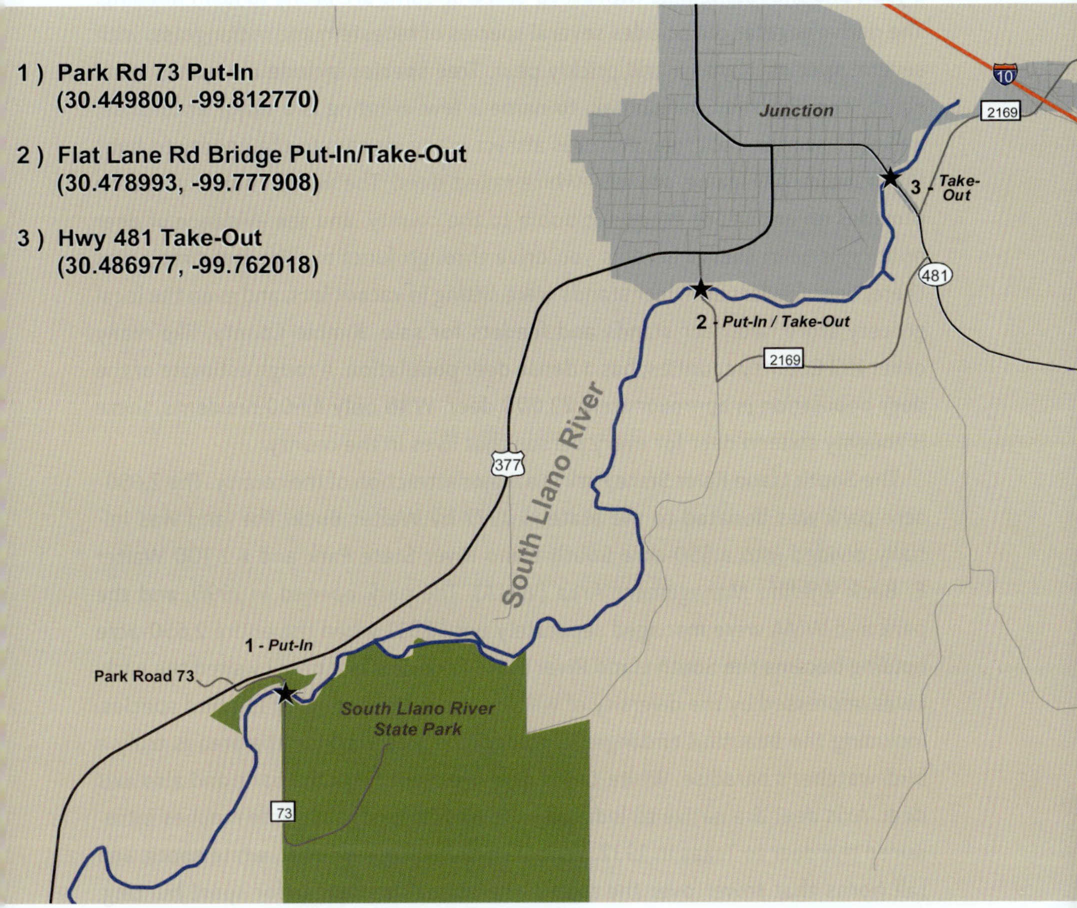


**FIGURE 8.32.** South Llano Paddling Trail

flows northeast across Edwards and Kimble Counties for approximately 55 miles. Just east of the city of Junction, it joins the North Llano River, and the two form the Llano River, which continues to flow east for another 100 miles until it empties into the Colorado River at Lake Lyndon B. Johnson.

Junction is the county seat of Kimble, with a population of around 2,500 residents. The county was created by the Texas legislature in 1858. It is named for Lieutenant George C. Kimble, a soldier who died in the Battle of the Alamo. Land use in the county is typical of the Texas Hill Country, with many farms and ranches that produce cattle, sheep, and goats. In fact, the county is one of the state's leading producers of wool and mohair. The land is characterized by rolling hills, with thin soils covering limestone. The rainfall averages around 23 inches a year, and the rolling hills with steep-sided streams are prone to flash flooding. The native vegetation includes several species of bluestem and indiangrass, with several species of yucca and prickly pear. Tree species include mesquite, cedar scrub, and live and Spanish oak, to name a few. Hunting is a major enterprise, and each winter, cool temperatures attract many visitors to the county to hunt the number one game animal—white-tailed deer. The winter hunting season provides an important economic boom to the county, and the evidence of deer hunting is seen everywhere as you drive through Junction. The last time I was there, deer feeders and deer stands were sitting in vacant lots, and even the local grocery store had deer stands and feeders for sale. Kimble County, like many other Hill Country counties, has a dense deer population. A rough estimate of the deer population is approximately 72,000 deer. With only 4,600 residents, there is roughly sixteen deer for every person that lives in the county.

The South Llano River State Park is a major attraction of the county. The 2,650-acre park was donated to the state in 1977 by Walter Buck. The land was initially divided into a 550-acre South Llano River State Park and a 2,100 Walter E. Buck Wildlife Management Area (WMA). The park opened in 1990, and the park and WMA were managed separately until 2011 when the entire 2,650-acre holding became the South Llano River State Park. The last time I visited the park, I was impressed by the diversity of wildlife I saw. With roughly 150 bird species, including the beautiful endangered golden-cheeked warbler, the area is truly a bird-watcher's paradise. White-tailed deer are plentiful in the park, and also axis deer. Axis deer are native to India and the Middle East, but game ranches introduced the deer to Texas in 1932. With its beautiful brown coat, white spots, and tall horns that tower over the males, the animal is popular for sport hunting. While axis deer were originally stocked on game ranches with deer-proof fences, escaped individuals established populations in surrounding areas. Today axis deer are free ranging in the county and across the Edwards Plateau. Because they are not considered a game animal, they can be hunted year-round, night or day. There is a large pecan bottomland near the river that has one of the largest winter roosting populations of Rio Grande turkeys anywhere. To protect the hundreds of turkeys that nest nearby, the park closes the area from October to April each year from 3:00 p.m. until 10:00 a.m. the following morning.

If you decide to visit the paddling trail, the park is a great place to stay. You can find primitive camps or take a camper, as I did on my last visit. There are approximately fifty sites that provide water and electricity. Campsites are surrounded by yucca, mesquite, oak, and cedar trees with a hard-surface pad to park on. There are restrooms and showers, and the park staff is very helpful.

***Put-in/Take-out*** The put-in for the 6-mile trail is in the South Llano River State Park. The launch is just inside the park entrance (30.449800 N, -99.812770 W). Approximately 4.7 miles downstream of the put-in is another access point at Flatrock Lane Crossing (30.478993 N, -99.777908 W). The trail take-out is at the Junction City Park (30.486977 N, -99.762018 W) on the north side of Junction Lake.

***Trail Description*** We left Austin on January 20, 2016, and traveled to South Llano River State Park. According to my GPS, the park is 150 miles from my house in Austin, and while that's a long way to travel to paddle a trail that is only 6 miles long, a stay in the park is worth the effort. There are great hiking and biking trails, and the north end of the park has approximately 2 miles of South Llano River frontage. The park also has a diverse avian fauna, which includes all three species of kingfishers: ringed, belted, and green.

We departed at around 9:00 a.m. and arrived at the park at approximately 12:30 p.m. The temperature was around 55 degrees. After parking our RVs, we ate lunch, took a bike ride through the park, cooked the evening meal, and turned in early. The next morning, we drove our shuttle vehicle to Junction and biked 5 miles back to the park.

Around 2:00 p.m., we launched our canoes at the Park Road 73 bridge. The water at the put-in is very shallow, and the river is only 30 to 40 feet wide (fig. 8.33). Once in our canoes, we followed the curves of the river and tried to stay in the faster-moving water. On the right side, steep banks rose up 10 to 15 feet, forming the north boundary of the park, while the rocky left bank sloped gently down to the water. Numerous rocks were scattered in the riverbed throughout this section of the river, along with the occasional shallow spot that tested our navigation skills. Our canoe has a flat bottom with no keel, so Joy and I skimmed over rocks, never needing to step out. Unfortunately, Brad and Colleen paddled an Alumacraft canoe with a keel. While the keel made the boat track better, it seemed to find every rock in the shallow stretches where the water was only 6 to 8 inches deep.

Approximately 0.65 miles from the launch is the Four-Mile Dam historic site. The only thing that remains of the dam is a concrete structure on the left side of the river (fig. 8.34).

The water's edge is lined with Baccharis and some bushy bluestem, with oak and pecan trees scattered along the banks. The deeper spots in the river are a beautiful dark blue distinguishable from the lighter shallows. There were cottonwoods here and there on the left bank and some mesquites on the park side. One of the first birds we saw on the river was a great blue heron. As we approached, it leisurely traveled downstream a few hundred yards and seemed to wait for us

**FIGURE 8.33.** The put-in near Park Road 73 at South Llano Paddling Trail

to catch up. It continued to lead the way down the river for the next 2 or 3 miles.

From time to time, the river channel is braided, which makes it difficult to know which channel to take. A large black and white bird with long, slender wings soared overhead; it was an osprey. The river was shallow, and we often bumped on rocks, but my wife and I never had to get out of our canoe.

Approximately 1.3 miles from the launch, several feral pigs ran from the left bank to the right. We only got a quick glimpse, but there were six or more adults and piglets in the group. As we paddled, there were spots where the river split and we chose the channel with the most flow.

At the halfway point, 3 miles down, we were surprised by a herd of deer running across the river. I tried to count them, but I am sure I missed some. To my amazement, I counted thirty-one. All were antlerless, and there were a few fawns in the group. That is the largest group of deer I have ever seen on any river.

At approximately mile 4, a large oak, rooted on the left bank, had fallen across the river. At first, we considered portaging, but we spotted a small passage at the base of the tree that we were able to paddle through.

As we continued, there were numerous small riffles and shallows, but we were able to paddle without major incident. While we bumped the bottom several times, we never run aground, and our feet were still dry at this point. Approximately 4.65 miles from the put-in is another access point at Flatrock Lane Bridge. As we approached the bridge, there was a rocky island in the middle of the river, and water flowed under the bridge near the bank on both sides. While it looked like there was a clear passage on either side, we chose the right because it seemed to have a better flow. However, once under the bridge, the river became shallow and Joy and I had to push off the bottom with our paddles to free ourselves. Our friends were not so lucky. Because of their keel, they had to get out and drag their craft through the shallows.

Approximately 5 miles from the launch, we saw another osprey perched in a tall tree. When we neared, the bird took off with what appeared to be a fish in his talons. Osprey feed almost exclusively on fish. As we continued to paddle, the river widened, and ahead we could see the long Highway 481 metal bridge that crosses the river. There was a great egret (fig. 8.35) standing near the left shoreline and a number of ducks up ahead. A cormorant ran across the water and then flew away. As we approached the bridge the ducks took off, but one bird stayed and dove under. When we got closer, the bird surfaced and I noticed a white patch near his bill; it was a blue-winged teal. He must have had an injury since he did not fly away with the others.

**FIGURE 8.34.** The remains of historic Four-Mile Dam on the South Llano River

**FIGURE 8.35.** A great egret standing in the shallows. Courtesy of Texas Parks and Wildlife Department

Sadly, our paddle was over. It took almost two hours, but we reached the take-out. As we paddled under the bridge, we saw our vehicle parked on the left bank in the city park. I can say that this section of the river was absolutely beautiful, and I observed a greater variety of wildlife on this paddling trail than any other I have paddled.

If you decide to paddle the South Llano Paddling Trail, I would recommend you call the park and check the flow. Because the river is spring fed, it has a flow year-round. When we paddled the river, the flow was 72 cubic feet per second at the Llano R.V. gauge near Junction. If flows are below this level, you may have to step out and walk through some shallows.

***Wildlife*** As I mentioned above, the wildlife viewing is outstanding in the park. In addition to my earlier description, we also saw a pied-billed grebe, fox squirrels, black vultures, an armadillo, white-winged doves, and numerous other passerine birds.

***Other Paddling Trails Nearby*** If you like this trail, you may want to try Nichol's Landing Paddling Trail. The trail is located approximately 105 miles southeast of Junction in Comal County. See the earlier section on "Nichol's Landing Paddling Trail." A second choice is the Saspamco Paddling Trail. The trail is approximately 145 miles southeast of Junction. The trail is a 12.1-mile meandering stream that is located just off Highway 1604 southeast of San Antonio.

I last paddled the Saspamco Paddling Trail on January 20, 2014, and the flow was great. Mourning and white-winged doves were everywhere, and one group of fifteen or more feral hogs crossed the river just in front of our canoes. If you choose to paddle the trail, I think you will enjoy it.

## Caddo Lake and Big Cypress Paddling Trails

### The Venue

In far northeast Texas on the Texas-Louisiana border is Caddo Lake. The 26,800-acre lake, known for its scenic habitat, and world's largest cypress forest, was designated a wetlands of worldwide importance in 1993 by the Ramsar Treaty. The treaty, signed at a convention in Iran in 1971, recognized over two thousand wetlands of worldwide significance. Caddo Lake is only one of thirteen Ramsar wetland sites in the United States.

The lake is named after the Caddo Indians who lived in the area until sometime in the nineteenth century. The origin of the lake is somewhat of a mystery. Some say that the lake was formed when flooding caused by a massive logjam, called the "Great Raft," dammed the Red River in Louisiana.[6] Some reports indicate that the logjam was 100 miles long.[7] The lake is unique because of its diverse flora and fauna. Biologists have identified 189 species of trees and shrubs, 216 species of birds, 90 fish, and many reptiles and mammals in the area.

Recognizing the importance of the area, the Texas Parks and Wildlife Department, in partnership with several local entities, created five paddling trails on the lake and five on Big Cypress Bayou adjacent to Caddo Lake (figs. 8.36 and 8.37). Caddo Lake is one of my favorite places to paddle because all the trails provide great scenery and bird-watching. Regrettably, the lake has experienced an infestation of an exotic aquatic plant that has changed the lake's character. In fact, there are sections of the lake that are so choked with giant Salvinia that paddling a canoe or kayak on certain trails may not be possible in the summer and fall.

Giant Salvinia is an invasive noxious plant that is native to Brazil and several other South American countries (see chapter 9). According to the Texas Parks and Wildlife Department (personal communication) the plant first appeared in the lake in 2006. Since that time, it has continued to spread over significant portions of all five paddling trails in the lake, making the trails challenging to paddle.

When I last visited in the fall of 2014, the giant Salvinia (fig. 8.38) had created a thick vegetative mat that covered the water's surface. In fact, three of the paddling trails (Carter's Chute, Cathedral, and Turtle Shell Paddling Trails) were so choked with the invasive plants that I could not paddle or pole my way through. I did paddle the Benton Lake and Old Folks Playground Paddling Trails, but both

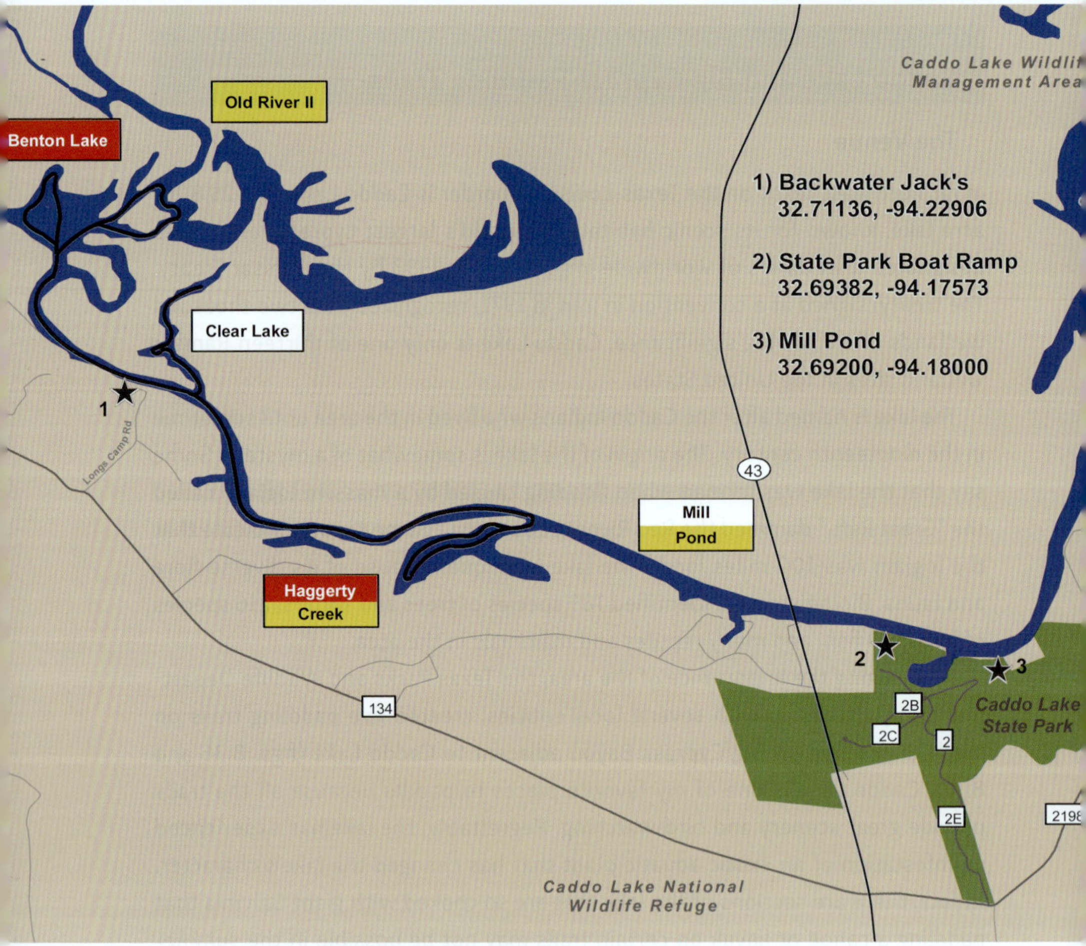


**FIGURE 8.36.** Big Cypress Paddling Trails

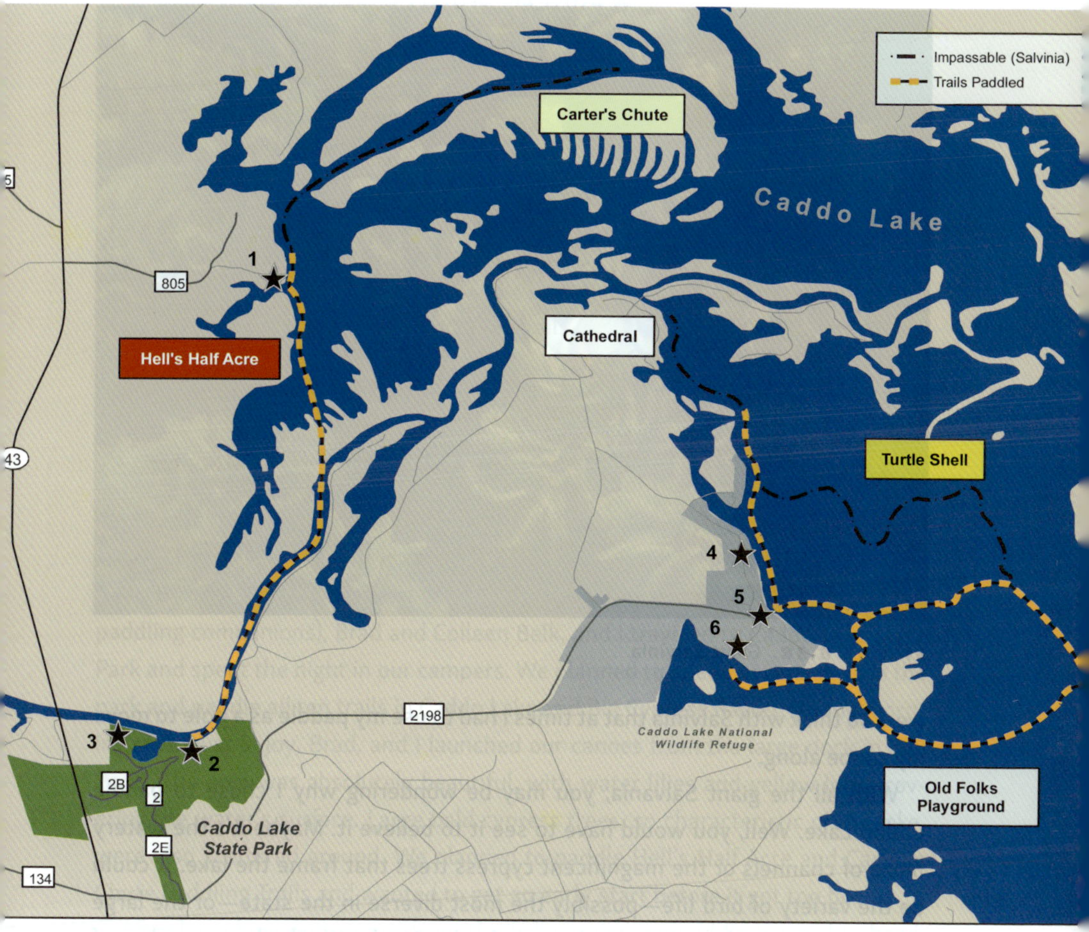


1) FM 805
32.73919, -94.16671

2) State Park Boat Ramp
32.69382, -94.17573

3) Mill Pond
32.69200, -94.18000

4) Shady Glade Resort
32.71270, -94.12024

5) Johnson's Ranch
32.70755, -94.11843

6) Crip's Camp
32.70242, -94.12227

**FIGURE 8.37.** Caddo Lake Paddling Trails

**FIGURE 8.39.** Color-coded directional signs for Caddo Lake and Big Cypress Bayou: (*a*) Benton Lake Paddling Trail, Big Cypress Bayou; (*b*) Clear Lake Paddling Trail, Big Cypress Bayou; (*c*) Haggerty Creek Paddling Trail, Big Cypress Bayou; (*d*) Mill Pond Paddling Trail, Big Cypress Bayou; (*e*) Old River II Paddling Trail, Big Cypress Bayou; (*f*) Carter's Chute Paddling Trail, Caddo Lake; (*g*) Cathedral Paddling Trail, Caddo Lake; (*h*) Hell's Half Acre Paddling Trail, Caddo Lake; (*i*) Old Folks Playground Paddling Trail, Caddo Lake; and (*j*) Turtle Shell Paddling Trail, Caddo Lake.

Courtesy of Texas Parks and Wildlife Department

g

h

i

j

vinia. Brad, in his solo boat, could not effectively paddle through the vegetation unless he stayed directly behind our tandem aluminum boat. If my wife and I pulled too far ahead of him, the path created by our canoe closed and Brad was stuck among the floating vegetation (fig. 8.41). Weary, but determined, we continued to paddle until we saw houses ahead. By then, we knew we had missed the take-out, but we all agreed, it was still time to pull out. Once on land, we realized that we were at a lodge that was closed; I can understand why. In hindsight, I can say that the paddling trail is unnavigable for recreational paddlers.

Once on land, I left my wife and Brad with the boats and walked about a mile to our car at the Caddo Lake Wildlife Management Area. After I drove back to pick up the rest of my party, we realized when we had passed the take-out for Hell's Half Acre Paddling Trail and had actually paddled the first part of Cater's Chute Paddling Trail. With little hesitation, we all agreed that Carter's Chute Paddling Trail was not an option for our afternoon paddle.

**FIGURE 8.40.** Giant Salvinia covering Hell's Half Acre Paddling Trail

After conferring over lunch, we decided to try another trail, but we wanted to find some open water free of vegetation. With this in mind, we tried the trails in Big Cypress Bayou. Mill Pond and Haggerty Creek Paddling Trails were the logical choice because they are nearby. Instead of paddling a loop course, we chose to drop a car off at the dock in the park and drive to Blackwater Jack's RV Park to launch our canoes. This time, Brad's wife, Colleen, decided to paddle with us, so they launched their tandem aluminum canoe. My wife and I stuck with our aluminum craft too. The launch site is right on the banks of Big Cypress Bayou. The channel is quite scenic, with bald cypress trees lining the shore. After paddling 1.85 miles down the bayou, we saw a red and yellow sign on our right that marks the entrance into Haggerty Creek.

Once in the creek, we followed the scenic trail for about ½ mile until it ended. We then turned around and traced our path back to Big Cypress Bayou. To continue our trip, we turned right and paddled down the bayou completing the Mill Pond Paddling Trail at the dock in Caddo Lake State Park where we had put-in that morning.

August 6—After a good night's rest, we returned to Backwater Jack's boat dock and paddled the remaining trails in the bayou: Benton Lake, Old River II, and Clear Lake Paddling Trails. All three trails are contiguous, and the total distance is about 8 or 9 miles.

At approximately nine, we launched our canoes in Big Cypress Bayou. After paddling less than a mile, we saw a red marker on our left for the entrance to Benton Lake. The channel opens into a lake with scattered bald cypress trees. Once in the lake, we wandered in between the large trees, circling to our left. The blue water and green cypress trees are stunning. Up ahead I could see several wood storks perched in the trees and a great blue heron in the shallow fringes of the lake (fig. 8.42). Have you ever watched a great blue heron fishing? The large bird stands still and statuesque in shallow water. When an unsuspecting fish swims too close, the spear-like bill of the bird finds its mark—end of story!

**FIGURE 8.41.** Brad suspended in a solid mat of giant Salvinia

**FIGURE 8.42.** Great blue heron standing in bald cypress trees in Benson Lake

After we made a complete circle to our left, we completed the Benton Lake Paddling Trail and were back to Big Cypress Bayou. We then turned left and continued upstream toward Old River II Paddling Trail. After paddling a short distance, we saw the entrance to the trail. As we paddled, the trail narrowed and wound through bald cypress trees. Up ahead a great egret stood in the shallow water. As we approached, it slowly flew farther up ahead and then circled back to the channel's entry point into Big Cypress Bayou. We paddled downstream to Blackwater Jack's RV Park, a distance of approximately 5 miles.

About 300 yards downstream from the boat ramp where we launched that morning, was the Clear Lake Paddling Trail. The channel is on the left side and is marked by a white sign with a black arrow and paddle. When we were in the channel, we zigzagged in and out of the trees, following the directional signs for a few hundred yards. We came to a berm with three metal culverts—the end of the trail. We turned around and returned to the large lake and paddled around the perimeter. Perched in a tree nearby were three white ibises. As we followed the perimeter, we paddled back into the Big Cypress Bayou and headed upstream a short distance to our take-out.

August 7—At approximately 8:30 a.m., we launched our canoes at the Shady Glade Resort on the west shoreline of Caddo Lake. There is a nominal $3 fee, but it is the best place to launch if you want to paddle the Cathedral Paddling Trail. Giant Salvinia was scattered along the shoreline, but we could see spots of open water, which gave us encouragement to try the trail. The area is beautiful, with looming cypress trees and yellow lotus scattered across the water's surface. We followed the trail, heading north, and paddled past Taylor Island on our left. Ahead the channel was nothing more than a narrow path where a motorboat had recently passed by. After a few hundred yards, the channel was completely choked with Salvinia again. With more than a mile to paddle before we reached the end of the trail, we opted to turn back. We knew we could intersect the Turtle Shell Paddling Trail if we retraced our path.

Alternating between paddling and poling our canoes back down the channel, we turned left (west) at a passage near Taylor Island and were on the Turtle Shell Paddling Trail. We were greeted not by an open waterway, but instead by a thick carpet of Salvinia. We had to concede that we could not paddle the 4.6-mile trail. Disappointed, we headed back to the put-in, but on the way, another channel crossed our path. We turned into it and for the first time we actually saw an opening to follow through the vegetation.

When we reached the shoreline, we were near another launch site called Johnson's Ranch. It was too early for lunch, so we set off to paddle the last remaining trail, Old Folks Playground Paddling Trail. This 4.9-mile trail is the southernmost trail in Caddo Lake and it shares its northern boundary with the Turtle Shell Trail.

From Johnson's Ranch, we headed east for approximately ½ mile and turned south to follow the trail down Starr Ditch. We could see open water with a clear path to paddle. Starr Ditch dead ended into a channel so we turned right (west) and headed to Crip's Camp. There was a solid stand of yellow lotus towering over our heads, forming a lush green and yellow forest around us (fig. 8.43). We followed the channel for approximately 0.6 miles to Crip's Camp. Crip's Camp is a private facility that is a launch site to enter the trail. When we reached the camp, we looked around, but apparently, the camp was closed. After lunch, we retraced our path on the water to the intersection with Starr Ditch. From there, we could see where Old Folks Playground Paddling Trail turned southeast and passed near Caddo Lake Wildlife National Management Area. After looking at our GPS, we learned that this was the southern portion of the trail, and if we followed it, we would circle back to Johnson's Ranch.

Because we wanted to complete the trail after all the disappointments we'd faced, we paddled on, knowing that we may have to pole our way through the Salvinia as we paddled farther onto the lake. We paddled southeast, then followed the trail north as it circled around Pine Island. We continued on the trail headed east toward our cars and the take-out. Three-quarters of a mile from the take-out, we encountered the Salvinia, and there was no clear way around it. We used our paddles to pole our way forward.

In the distance, we heard a motorboat and, I must admit, I wished at that moment I had a motor on my canoe. As the sound of the motor approached, I saw it was an airboat, and as it drew nearer, we recognized the driver as someone we'd met earlier that morning when we were trying to find the Turtle Shell Trail.

**FIGURE 8.43.** Yellow lotus line the Old Folks Paddling Trail in route to Crip's Camp. Courtesy of Brad Belk

Flagging him down, we asked if he would drive down the trail in front of us and open a path in the Salvinia. He agreed.

As the boat sped ahead, vegetation and water flew everywhere, leaving us frantically paddling as fast as we could through the path that had briefly materialized. We could see familiar landmarks and knew we were near shore and our take-out at Shady Glade Resort.

On shore, we were happy that we completed the trail, but we were glad to be back on dry land. Regrettably, we could not paddle three of the trails in the lake: Cathedral, Turtle Shell, and Carter's Chute Paddling Trails. The trails in Big Cypress Bayou are a great place to paddle, but I would recommend that you call Caddo Lake State Park and check the status of the trails before driving there. You may want to consider paddling in the spring, because cooler weather during the winter retards and kills the plant's growth.

The following summer, I contacted staff at the Texas Parks and Wildlife Department to check on the trails and the condition of the giant Salvinia. According to Tim Bister, a fisheries biologist with Texas Parks and Wildlife Department, the infestation of Salvinia is still a significant problem. In fact, a survey conducted by the department revealed that Salvinia has spread from approximately 2,400 acres to 2,800 acres from the previous year. On the bright side, he did mention that the Texas Parks and Wildlife Department is continuing research on the plant and spraying herbicide to keep the boat lanes open.

I learned from Lee Eisenberg that original research was conducted by Texas A&M on a weevil that eats the plant, but regrettably the research was stopped when money ran out. More recently, the Greater Caddo Lake Association, the City of Uncertain, and other local entities raised money to continue research on the weevil. Mr. Eisenberg stated that he is involved with a program to control and hopefully eradicate the plant by raising weevils. He further indicated that 100,000 weevils were released in 2015. While some preliminary results look favorable, only time will tell how successful the program will be.

***Wildlife*** Caddo Lake, with its maze of bayous, sloughs, and magnificent 400-year-old cypress trees, provides a wealth of habitat not only for water birds but also for all types of wildlife. In addition to the species mentioned above, I also saw a Louisiana heron, a belted kingfisher, snowy egrets, a red-eared turtle, black vultures, and a number of species of passerine birds. The lake has one of the highest breeding populations of wood ducks; it is home to several threatened or rare species like the peregrine falcon and the alligator snapping turtle. There are eighteen species of game fish; other common species include beaver, nutria, raccoon, mink, squirrel, armadillo, and white-tailed deer, to name a few.

***Other Paddling Trails Nearby*** Approximately 80 miles west of Caddo Lake is another paddling trail, Mineola Bigfoot Paddling Trail, located on the Sabine River, just south of Mineola. This 11.9-mile trail meanders east from the US 69 put-in to the FM 1804 boat ramp take-out. If you choose to camp, there is a public camping area on the north side of the river, 5 miles from the put-in. The site has picnic tables and a gravel area for tents and sleeping bags. The campsite is part of a larger 3,000-acre Mineola Nature Preserve owned by the city of Mineola. There are hiking and biking trails and fishing ponds in the area, should you choose to spend more time there.

A second paddling trail, located approximately 100 miles south-southwest of Caddo Lake, is the Neches–Davy Crockett Paddling Trail. The 9.2-mile trail follows the Neches River in a south-southeasterly direction. The paddling trail begins approximately 25 miles northwest of the town of Lufkin. The trail put-in is at the CR 1155 crossing of the Neches River, and the take-out is downstream at the Highway 7 crossing of the river.

## COASTAL PADDLING TRAILS

When the first paddling trail was completed in 1999, little did anyone know that the trail system would grow to one of the most active in the country. Scattered along the coast from the most northern, Galveston Island State Paddling Trail, to the most southern, South Bay Paddling Trail, the coastal trails give Texans a chance to paddle, bird-watch, fish, and enjoy different areas of the coast. I hope you visit a trail in your area. In the following section, I have provided information on two of my favorite coastal trails.

### Lighthouse Lakes Paddling Trail

#### The Venue

Redfish Bay is located on the mid-Texas coast near the town of Aransas Pass. This 50-square-mile saltwater bay has a number of diverse coastal habitats, including mangroves, seagrass flats, sand flats, oyster reefs, and other aquatic vegetation that provides important nursery habitat for many sport and shellfish. The bay, with its abundant fish fauna, is one of the most popular sport fishing sites along the Texas coast. One unique feature of the bay is its 14,000 acres of seagrass beds, which comprise five species: star grass, manatee grass, shoal grass, widgeon grass, and turtle grass. Fragile, submerged seagrasses provide cover and food for invertebrate and smaller prey fish that are an important food source for many sport fish.

Recognizing the importance of the habitat and its recreational opportunities, the Texas Parks and Wildlife Department chose this area to create the first state paddling trail in 1999. The portion of the bay chosen is bordered by the Corpus Christi Channel on the west, Lydia Ann Channel on the east, Aransas Channel on the south, and Quarantine Shore on the north. Each year many visitors come to the area to view the abundant shorebirds and migrant birds from paddle boats that allow paddlers to get a closer look without scaring the birds.

***Put-in/Take-out*** When the Lighthouse Lakes Paddling Trail (fig. 8.45) was dedicated in 1999, two public points of access bordered Highway 361, which leads from Aransas Pass to Port Aransas.

When I last visited the trail in October 2015, to my surprise one access point, Crabman Marina, was replaced by the Aransas Queen Casino. When I pulled into the parking lot, I noticed a large ship anchored near the shore, and there were a number of cars parked in the dirt lot—none of the cars had kayaks tied on top. I knew immediately that something had changed. When I inquired in the office, I learned that the lot had been acquired by a new owner and the ship was a floating casino that takes trips out each day.

Because the site is no longer a public access point, paddlers will need to travel to the Lighthouse Lakes Park that is located about 0.8 miles farther down Highway 361 on the way to Port Aransas.

Lighthouse Lakes Park—The park is located approximately 4.8 miles from the H-E-B market in Aransas Pass (27.86216 N, -97.07589 W). It's a great place to put-in and paddle Cutters Trail, or you can also intersect the other three trails from Cutters Trail.

There is a parks department sign on the left side as you drive down Highway 361 and a kiosk that describes the trail. The park is small, but there is plenty of parking space along the shore, and a hard surface road runs parallel to Highway 361. Two small, covered, overlook pavilions are near the shore along with several shaded, rustic picnic tables. You only have to carry your boat a short distance to put-in on the sand beach. Aransas Channel runs along the shore; you will have to paddle across the deep channel to the first trail marker, #60, where the Cutters Trail begins. Watch out for large recreation and commercial boats that travel down the channel.

## Lydia Ann Lighthouse

A unique feature of the bay, Lydia Ann Lighthouse (fig. 8.44) overlooks Lydia Ann channel near the town of Port Aransas. Designated as a National Historic Monument, the lighthouse dates back to the Civil War. In 1861, Confederate forces hid the lens from the lighthouse in the marsh so the Union forces could not use it.[1] Unfortunately, the location of the lens was lost and is still missing to this day. Two years later, in 1863, the Confederate troops blew the top 20 feet off the tower, which was later rebuilt after the war. The lighthouse was decommissioned in 1952 and sold for $25,000 to Everett Bohls in 1955. In 1973, Charles Butt, founder of the H-E-B grocery chain, purchased it. During the next ten years, the lighthouse and buildings nearby were restored. Still in private ownership today by the Butt family, it continues to tower over the bay. While the lighthouse no longer guides ships to shore, it does provide a good landmark for paddlers who may get disorientated while paddling through the maze of mangroves scattered throughout the trail.

1. Jeremy D'Entremont, "Texas's 'Lydia Ann' Shines On," *Lighthouse Digest*, May 2007, 12.

**FIGURE 8.44.** Lydia Ann Lighthouse

Harbor Island Road—Located less than ½ mile from Lighthouse Lakes Paddling Trail is a second access point, Harbor Island Road (27.860072 N, -97.076748 W). The road is on the left side of Highway 361 and runs parallel to the highway. When you drive past Lighthouse Lakes Trails Park sign and proceed toward Port Aransas, there is a bridge immediately past the park. Once you cross the bridge, in about 50 yards, turn left and travel a short distance to where the road "T's." Turn right and continue for about 150 yards to a small sand put-in. You can see trail marker sign #1 immediately across the wide, deep-water channel. This is where the Redfish Loop Trail begins. There is no parking lot, so most boaters and fishermen park along the road.

**FIGURE 8.45.** Lighthouse Lakes Paddling Trails

***Trail Description*** Of all the coastal trails, the Lighthouse Lakes Trails are my absolute favorite on the coast because they have many inviting features: good access, unique habitats, excellent bird-watching, great fishing, and a historic lighthouse. A paddler can meander through the area and travel from one trail to the other because they are interconnected. You can paddle a short trail like the 1.25-mile Electric Lake Loop, longer trails like the 5-mile Cutters Loop, the 6.7-mile South Bay Loop, or the 6.8-mile Redfish Loop. You can also explore the area by picking a different route that connects one or more trails.

Unlike inland trails that follow a stream or river, coastal trails do not always follow a channel, but sometimes wander through open water areas. In order to mark the path of the trail, numbered signs are placed in the water. Each marker is a square sign mounted on a white PVC pipe (fig. 8.46). The location of each sign has corresponding GPS coordinates that mark the path of the trail. While it is possible to paddle the trail without a GPS receiver or a map of the coordinates, I recommend using at least one or both. You cannot always see each sign as

**FIGURE 8.46.** Trail marker #59

## Redfish Bay State Scientific Area

While seagrass was once abundant along the Texas coast, it is disappearing from the area.[1] The Texas Parks and Wildlife Department designated the entire bay as the Redfish Bay State Scientific Area in 2006 in an attempt to prevent the loss of seagrass, which is vulnerable to motorboat traffic. Motorboat propellers uproot vegetation, and the scars persist for years, preventing new growth. Regulations prohibit the uprooting and digging out of seagrass plants and carries a misdemeanor offense and fine ranging from $25 to $500. Hopefully, this action will allow the recolonization of more seagrass in the future.

---

1. Texas Parks and Wildlife Department, "Seagrass Conservation Plan for Texas, 1999," Austin, TX, 1999, 35.

they may be missing or hidden in the mangroves. The trail markers can be distinguished from other markers by their distinctive square white signs with large orange numbers on the white background. A list of the GPS points for the trails is found later in this section.

The Aransas Channel is a deepwater channel so be careful and watch for tug boats, barges, and other large commercial and recreational crafts. These boats can cause large wakes that could flip your boat. Also, because of the inherent dangers of paddling an open canoe in coastal water, only kayaks are recommended for this trail.

The first trail marker for Cutters Trail can be seen from the shore, but you must paddle across the Aransas Channel to enter the trail. The trail is actually a loop that follows an irregular circle with markers numbered 44, 43, 39, 40, 62, 63, 64, 65, 24, 10, 47, and then back to 60.

If you want to paddle the 6.7 South Bay Loop Trail, you have two options. You can either paddle northwest up the Aransas Channel to marker #59, where the trail begins, or you can access the South Bay Loop Trail by paddling the Cutters Trail. For that route, once you get to marker #40, follow markers numbered 57, 53, 51, 50, 35, and then paddle back to #40. This trail has lots of open water and is not as scenic as the other three trails. If you choose to paddle Redfish Loop or Electric Lake Loop Trails and would like to go to the Lydia Ann Lighthouse you may choose to put-in at the Harbor Island Road Access.

From there you will again have to paddle across the deep Aransas Channel. The first marker for the Redfish Loop Trail is immediately across the channel and is visible from the put-in. From marker #1 paddle to numbers 2, 8, 9, 10, and at #47 you will cross Cutters Trail. Continue to paddle to numbers 44, 42, 41, 36, 33, 30, 28, 26, 20, 21, 12, 13, and 14. At this point you can see the Lydia Ann Lighthouse; it is clearly visible east of marker #14. To paddle to the lighthouse, follow the channel that wanders through the mangroves. Once you have paddled to the lighthouse, you can complete the Redfish Loop trail by paddling back to marker #14, then to numbers 15, 7, and 6. Just past marker #6 is where the Electric Loop Trail begins. To access the trail, turn east and watch for marker #4 and continue to paddle east to marker #61. From this point, paddle south then west and make a circle, ending back at #5, then back to #4 to complete the short 1.25-mile trail. Continue to paddle west to #3 and then back to #1 where you began. As I mentioned, a map and GPS receiver are recommended. Laminated color maps of this trail complex that include the GPS coordinates are available from some retailers. Contact Shoreline Publishing (http://www.shorelineaerialmaps.com/photo-prints.htm) by calling 713–973–1627 to get a list of local retailers.

***Safety Considerations*** Unlike inland paddling trails, coastal trails have several inherent hazards that you should be aware of. Because coastal trails have shallow water areas, it is important to check the tides when planning your trip. Information on the tides can be obtained at http://tidesandcurrents.noaa.gov/stations.html?type=Water+Levels. Some areas of coastal trails are too shallow to paddle when the tide is out, and dragging your boat can be difficult, especially in muddy areas or areas where oyster reefs are found. Oyster reefs are scattered throughout some coastal trails, and the sharp shell clusters can cut your shoes and damage your boat. Shoes with good soles are recommended rather than soft-soled water shoes. Always check the weather before you go paddling because strong winds can blow your boat around and waves or swells can flip your boat. If possible, plan to paddle with other boats or paddle with a partner in a tandem kayak. When strong winds are blowing, care should be taken when paddling across open water areas. Unless you are an expert paddler or have a guide who knows the trail, I would not recommend an open canoe on this trail. Kayaks are a better choice. Wind and waves can swamp open canoes and make paddling conditions difficult.

Trail Marker Numbers and GPS Coordinates for Lighthouse Lakes Paddling Trails:

1. 27.86216 N, -97.07589 W
2. 27.86527 N, -97.07335 W
3. 27.86431 N, -97.07169 W
4. 27.86244 N, -97.06867 W
5. 27.86092 N, -97.06664 W
6. 27.86430 N, -97.06758 W
7. 27.86378 N, -97.06585 W
8. 27.86780 N, -97.07218 W
9. 27.08645 N, -97.07155 W
10. 27.86921 N, -97.07023 W
12. 27.86706 N, -97.06299 W
13. 27.86567 N, -97.06277 W
14. 27.86499 N, -97.06154 W
15. 27.86311 N, -97.06145 W
20. 27.87085 N, -97.05764 W
21. 27.87028 N, -97.06001 W
24. 27.87374 N, -97.06213 W
26. 27.87988 N, -97.05530 W
28. 27.88470 N, -97.05583 W
30. 27.88863 N, -97.05589 W
33. 27.89466 N, -97.06045 W
35. 27.89408 N, -97.07041 W
36. 27.88733 N, -97.07873 W
39. 27.88126 N, -97.07873 W
40. 27.88184 N, -97.08015 W
41. 27.88177 N, -97.07169 W
42. 27.88041 N, -97.07314 W
43. 27.87751 N, -97.07487 W
44. 27.87604 N, -97.07645 W
47. 27.87067 N, -97.07226 W
48. 27.88964 N, -97. 08119 W
50. 27.89690 N, -97.07453 W
51. 27.90681 N, -97.06789 W
53. 27.91230 N, -97.07662 W
57. 27.89626 N, -97.08817 W
59. 27.87534 N, -97.09009 W

| | |
|---|---|
| 60. 27.86906 N, -97.08342 W | 63. 27.88348 N, -97.06626 W |
| 61. 27.86059 N, -97.06298 W | 64. 27.87978 N, -97.06470 W |
| 62. 27.88557 N, -97.06584 W | 65. 27.87885 N, -97.06355 W |

***Wildlife*** If you are a bird-watcher, the variety and number of birds found in this area are phenomenal. In fact, Nueces County has been referred to as the "Birdest Coastal County" in Texas. Like all coastal counties there is an abundance of shorebirds, and migrant species also frequent the area each year. Like in most coastal counties, you could expect to see gulls, terns, wading birds, and pelicans. I have several favorites that I always look for, in particular the roseate spoonbill, American avocet, black-necked stilt, and black skimmer. Skimmers are one of my favorites. They have such striking black and white coloration with black wings, tail, back, and the top of their head. In contrast, their breast, face, and neck are white. It almost looks like they are wearing a tuxedo. Another unique feature is their elongated reddish and black-tipped bill. While the top beak is long and narrow, the lower beak is even longer and sticks out several inches past the top beak.

With this elongated lower mandible, skimmers have a unique way of feeding. They feed mostly at night, but I have seen them flying in daylight just inches above the water surface with the lower bill submerged in the water. With their long graceful wings, they fly inches above the water and skim up small fish, insects, and crustaceans from the water (fig. 8.47).

**FIGURE 8.47.** Black skimmer.
Courtesy of Texas Parks and Wildlife Department

In addition to a thriving bird population, the area is one of the most popular fishing areas along the Texas coast. If you choose to try your hand at fishing from a kayak, speckled trout, red drum, and black drum are plentiful in the area.

***Other Paddling Trails Nearby*** If you want to try your hand at another coastal paddling trail, a couple are nearby. If you drive south on Highway 361 from the Lighthouse Lakes Paddling Trails complex only a few miles, you can take the ferry across the Corpus Christi Channel to the town of Port Aransas. Continue to follow 361 about 13 miles down Mustang Island to Fish Pass (27.73744 N, -97.13750 W), where the Mustang Island Paddling Trails begin. Fish Pass is a popular put-in for both motorized boats and kayaks and is only a short paddle out into Corpus Christi Bay. There are also two additional access points along the trails; you can choose to paddle one or more trails that vary in length from 5.2 to 8.5 miles. The majority of the trail complex follows the shoreline of Corpus Christi Bay, but portions wind through the cuts and small bayous.

Less than a mile from Fish Pass is Mustang Island State Park. The 4,000-acre park and island are named for the wild horses (mustangs) that once roamed the island. The park has beachfront on the Gulf of Mexico and has electric hookups with water and primitive camping. It is a great place to camp or hang out before or after you paddle the trails.

The Port O'Connor Paddling Trail, is located approximately 85 miles north of the Lighthouse Lakes Trail, in the town of Port O'Connor. Highway 185 terminates in Port O'Connor in Calhoun County. Two access points to the trail in the town are located along the Intracoastal Waterway. The best place to launch is the Fishing Center (28.43863 N, -96.41402 W). There is a nominal fee to use the ramp, but it is the best place to launch. You can also launch free of charge at Froggie's Bait Dock (28.43863333 N, -96.41401667 W) at the end of Bayer Street in Port O'Connor; it is ½ mile from Fisherman's Cut, where the trail begins. Both access points border the Intracoastal Waterway, and you have to cross the channel to reach trail marker #1. The Intracoastal Waterway serves large commercial boats and barges so be careful crossing the channel.

The trail complex is made up of six trails (25, 11, 8, 13, 16, and 17 miles) that are interconnected. Various routes meander through the bayous, open water, and follow the shoreline of Espiritu Santo Bay. The trails terminate on Matagorda Island, a 38-mile barrier that borders Espiritu Santo Bay. The island is a Wildlife Management Area managed by the Texas Parks and Wildlife Department (TPWD) and is free for day use.

The island was once a military training facility and has a cast iron lighthouse that was originally built in 1852. Storms and beach erosion damaged the 55-foot lighthouse, and in 1857 it was relocated and the light tower was raised 24 feet. During the Civil War, the lighthouse was again damaged by confederate forces to keep it out of Union hands. In 1873, it was rebuilt to a height of 92 feet at a new site. More recently the Texas Parks and Wildlife Department restored the lighthouse at considerable cost, more than one million dollars.[8]

As I mentioned earlier, day use is permissible at no cost, but if you plan to camp overnight, you will need to get a Limited Public Use Permit. Permits are available at TPWD license offices or online. For more information, contact the local Office of TPWD at 361-205-1510.

## Armand Bayou Paddling Trail

### The Venue

Located just a short drive from Houston near the city of Pasadena is a small bayou that flows into Mud Lake. The bayou, originally called Middle Bayou, was renamed Armand Bayou by the city of Pasadena in the 1970s. The area is unique because although urban growth and industrial development have spread, the land near the bayou has remained relatively pristine. The area is a mixture of coastal marsh, tall grass prairie, and riparian woods. This lush environment provides an excellent habitat for wildlife, especially birdlife. Over 220 species of birds have been reported in the area. One of the most visible residents is the American alligator (fig. 8.48). Over the years, I have seen a number of gators while paddling the trail, some over 10 feet long.

***Put-in/Take-out*** There are several launch points along Armand Bayou Paddling Trail (fig. 8.49). Depending on how long you want to paddle, you can do the entire 8.2-mile trail or only a portion of it. Normally the flow in the bayou is little to none, so you can easily paddle upstream or downstream and then return to your launch site. One of the most popular launch sites is the Bay Area Park (29.59553 N, -95.08979 W) located at 7500 Bay Area Boulevard, Houston, Texas, 77058. The park is 5.4 miles from the I-45 exit and has a dock for launching your boat along with restrooms, picnic tables, plenty of parking, and other amenities should you choose to have lunch or spend more time there.

A second launch site is located at Clear Lake Park at 5001 East NASA Road, Seabrook, TX, 77586 (29.58827 N, -95.07018 W). This park is 5 miles from the I-45 exit. The 59-acre Harris County Park is the beginning point for the trail; it has plenty of parking, picnic tables, playground equipment, a kids' play area, a pavilion, and other amenities. The first trail marker, #1 (29.56627 N, -95.07018

**FIGURE 8.48.** American alligator.
Courtesy of Texas Parks and Wildlife Department

W), is located near the fishing pier. If you choose to launch there, you can follow the entire trail, but unless you drop a vehicle at Bay Area Park or the launch point on Red Bluff Road, you will have to paddle all the way back to the put-in. The park is open during the day year-round (713-274-7275).

A third launch site is located on Big Island Slough, where it flows under Red Bluff Road. The physical address is 9800 Red Bluff Road (29.613254 N, -95.084746 W). If you travel southwest on Red Bluff Road, the launch is located on the right side as you approach Big Island Slough. There is a small parking area and a small cement pad down on the slough to launch your boat. Paddle south on the bayou and you will enter Armand Bayou between trail markers #19 and #20.

*Trail Description* The trail begins at Clear Lake Park, located on NASA Road 1. The first trail marker #1 is near the fishing pier in the park on the east bank of Mud Lake. If you enjoy fishing from your boat, Mud Lake is a mixing zone for fresh and saltwater. As you follow the trail, you will pass by markers numbered 2, 3, and 4 on the west bank of the lake. Once you pass marker #4, no gasoline-powered boats are allowed; only paddle craft and boats with electric trolling motors are legal beyond this point, making for a quiet, peaceful paddle. As you continue to paddle upstream, the lake narrows and you will see marker

## Armand Bayou Nature Center

Located on the banks of Armand Bayou is a 2,500-acre area known as Armand Bayou Nature Center. If you choose to paddle the Armand Bayou Paddling Trail, I would highly recommend a visit to the center. It is recognized as one of the largest urban wilderness preserves in the United States. The nature center and the bayou are named after a local conservationist, Armand Yramategui. Mr. Yramategui was curator of the Burke Baker Planetarium and an environmental activist who worked diligently to protect the area from development. Tragically, he lost his life in a freeway robbery and murder in 1970. Following his death, several local individuals, especially Mrs. Hana Ginzbarg, and conservation organizations continued to oppose development near the bayou and a proposed flood control project that would have modified the bayou. After several years' work by local individuals and with funding from the city of Pasadena and some federal funding, the land near the bayou was purchased and saved from development. Finally, in 1974 the Armand Bayou Nature Center was founded.

I will never forget the first time I visited the center. It was in 1978, long before the creation of the Armand Bayou Paddling Trail. Back then I worked for the Texas Air Control Board, and I came to assist and monitor a "prescribed burn" that was planned for a portion of the prairie. While these burns are a common tool of habitat management, due to the center's location in the middle of urban development, a burn is not a common practice. Consequently, to ensure that the burn did not spread to the surrounding area, firefighters, law enforcement officials, county and city employees, staff from the center, and a number of volunteers monitored the burn. There were even media representatives present, and a helicopter flew overhead to oversee the action.

I was positioned on a road, and as the fire approached, it gave off lots of heat. The burning dead grass and small brush made a loud crackling noise. Shortly before the fire reached the road, the wildlife that were hiding in the ground cover began to run across the road to escape the heat. There were lots of cotton rats, rabbits, several snakes, mice, and other rodents trying to get away from the fire. One cotton rat actually ran across my foot when it tried to escape. It was quite a sight to see the mass exodus of animals running from the fire. At the end of the day, the fire had blackened the landscape; it burned itself out without incident.

The area remains relatively unchanged. The nature center has a full-time staff that provides environmental and interpretive programs, with exhibits of live animals and projects that feature habitat restoration. A boardwalk winds through the forest and marsh, and nature trails extend over 5 miles. The area boasts a diverse fauna, including more than 370 species of birds, mammals, reptiles, and amphibians.

The center offers monthly guided canoe trips on the bayou; pontoon boat tours are offered on Saturdays on the *Bayou Ranger*. The center is located at 8500 Bay Area Boulevard, Pasadena, TX, 77507, telephone 281-474-2551.

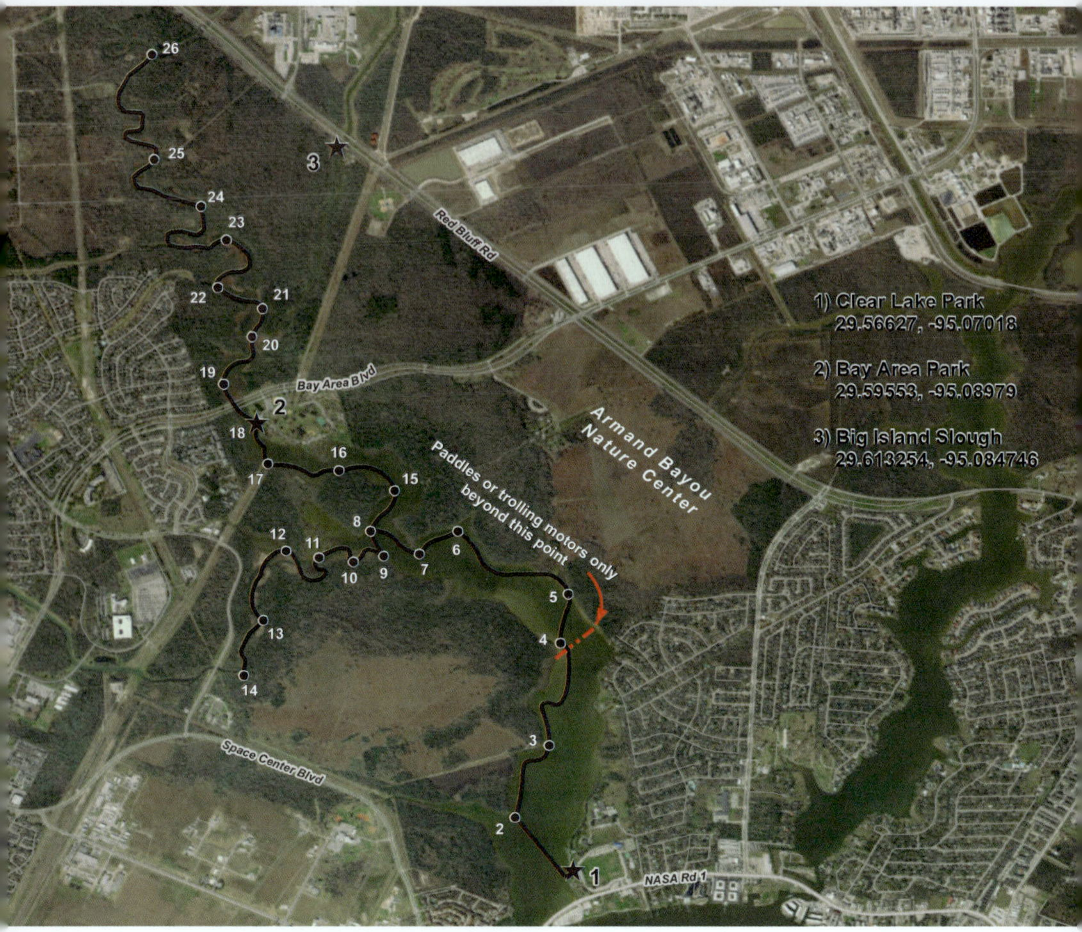


**FIGURE 8.49.** Armand Bayou Paddling Trail

#5 on the east shoreline. As you continue to paddle the trail, follow the shoreline until you reach trail marker #7. At this point you will need to decide which fork of the trail you want to take. If you want to paddle the entire trail, take the left fork, which is Horsepen Bayou. You will see trail marker #8 on the right bank and #9 on the left bank. Continue to follow the channel and you will see marker #10 up ahead. As you continue to paddle up the bayou, the channel winds around, and at times there are small islands. If you follow the main channel you will eventually reach markers numbered 11, 12, and 13, with the channel ending at marker #14. If you continue to paddle past marker #14, you will see Middlebrook Drive Bridge, crossing the bayou. At this point turn around and retrace your path back to the mouth of Horsepen Bayou. Then, turn left at marker #8 and proceed up Armand Bayou toward marker #15. As you proceed up Armand Bayou you will see marker #16 near the left bank, and just ahead on the right bank is Bay Area Park. The park is a popular launch site, and if you take-out here you have paddled 5.5 miles. If you continue on, you will pass marker #18 and paddle under Bay Area Boulevard. Once under the boulevard, bear left around a small island and stay left. On the right is a small tributary, Big Island Slough. If you paddle up Big Island Slough to Red Bluff Road there is another launch site.

After you pass Big Island Slough, continue up Armand Bayou past markers #20 and #21, at this point the bayou begins to twist and turn as it narrows down to the trail's end at marker #26. At this point, you have paddled 8.2 miles, and this is where the paddling trail ends. Once you turn around, you can either retrace your path back to the Clear Lake Park or take-out at an alternate launch at Red Bluff Road or Bay Area Park.

On my last visit in July 2015, to my surprise, water hyacinth was scattered throughout the trail. This (fig. 8.50) invasive, noxious, exotic plant is native to the Amazon Basin of South America (see chapter 9). While I had seen this plant in other river systems, I had not seen it on this trail in large concentrations.

**FIGURE 8.50.** Water hyacinth in Armand Bayou near trail marker #6

When I launched my canoe near trail marker #1, I could see floating mats of the plant scattered in Mud Lake. The plants did not impede my progress, but there were areas along the trail where thick mats were floating near the bank. One of the largest concentrations of the plant was along the bank near the boat dock in Bay Area Park.

While at the site, I had a chance to visit with Mark Kramer, stewardship coordinator for Armand Bayou Nature Center. According to Mark, the plant has become a real problem. In fact, he mentioned that the recent rains had washed many of the floating plants out of the bayou and into Mud Lake. Prior to the rains, the plants had been even worse. While paddling the trail, I noticed an airboat that was spraying the plant with herbicide. Hopefully the spraying will keep the plant under control. If you plan to paddle the trail, I would recommend that you contact the nature center to check on the status of water hyacinth.

Trail Marker Numbers and GPS Coordinates for Armand Bayou Paddling Trail:

1. 29.56627 N, -95.07018 W
2. 29.5704 N, -95.07392 W
3. 29.57477 N, -95.07148 W
4. 29.58116 N, -95.0705 W
5. 29.58489 N, -95.07022 W
6. 29.58885 N, -95.07709 W
7. 29.58751 N, -95.07986 W
8. 29.58859 N, -95.08292 W
9. 29.58707 N, -95.08179 W
10. 29.58671 N, -95.08379 W
11. 29.587 N, -95.08559 W
12. 29.58736 N, -95.08800 W
13. 29.58286 N, -95.08959 W
14. 29.57966 N, -95.0909 W
15. 29.59116 N, -95.08131 W
16. 29.5925 N, -95.08451 W
17. 29.59292 N, -95.08932 W
18. 29.59553 N, -95.08979 W
19. 29.60022 N, -95.09206 W
20. 29.60022 N, -95.09039 W
21. 29.60248 N, -95.08946 W
22. 29.6043 N, -95.0926 W
23. 29.60744 N, -95.09184 W
24. 29.60934 N, -95.09317 W
25. 29.61237 N, -95.09602 W
26. 29.61893 N, -95.09653 W

***Wildlife*** Because the bayou is a mixing zone for salt- and freshwater, there is a diversity of habitats for wildlife. As previously mentioned, 220 species of birds have been recorded in the area. Pelicans, herons, gulls, and terns are common. You may even see a roseate spoonbill or an osprey.

On a previous visit to the trail, I spotted an osprey perched on a dead tree. Ospreys are beautiful black and white hawks that feed almost exclusively on fish. As I approached the hawk in my canoe, it flew away. I thought I had spooked it, but I soon realized that the bird was feeding. When the bird flew by, it swooped down closer to the water with its talons open. Then it crashed into the water and immediately flew up with a fish in its talons and landed in a nearby tree. This

**FIGURE 8.51.** An osprey with a meal of largemouth bass in its talons.
Courtesy of Texas Parks and Wildlife Department

magnificent bird with a five-and-a-half-foot wingspan, had just caught food for the day (fig. 8.51).

If you paddle the trail you may also see alligators, especially if you paddle the upper reaches of Horsepen Bayou or Armand Bayou near markers #21 through #26. I know that some paddlers may not want to paddle where alligators are found, and I can understand that. However, I have observed that when I approach an alligator in my boat, they always swim away or submerge underwater. I have never had an encounter or witnessed aggressive behavior by alligators.

I have learned that eighteen known fatalities have been documented in the United States from alligator attacks in the past sixty-seven years. With the exception of one fatality in Georgia, all other fatalities were in Florida, and no fatalities were recorded in the report in Texas. However, a recent fatality occurred that changed that. On July 3, 2015, a twenty-eight-year-old man was killed while swimming in a bayou in Orange County, Texas. Reportedly, the man ignored warnings by friends not to go swimming. The fatality occurred near a restaurant that fed scraps to alligators. According to a nationwide database, which dates back to 1948, most attacks resulted from activities such as swimming, fishing, or retrieving golf balls. So, stay in your boats and no swimming allowed.[9]

During the past fifteen years, I have paddled the trail on many occasions in a kayak and a canoe, and while I have not witnessed any aggressive behavior from alligators, I do think all paddlers should take several precautions when paddling in areas where alligators are found.

A few recommended precautions include:

- Never go swimming.
- If you put-in or take-out along the bayou in areas where tall grass occurs, inspect the area before you walk on the grass to make sure there are no gators nesting or sleeping.
- If you have a dog along, make sure they are on a leash anytime you are near the water.
- If you approach a gator on the bank or in the water, paddle away and do not harass or pester it.
- In areas of the bayou that are narrow, paddle in the center of the bayou (not up against the bank) since resting or sleeping gators may launch from the bank right beside you.
- While I do feel that most recreational boats are inherently stable and safe to paddle in areas where alligators are found, I would not recommend a stand-up paddleboard in the bayou. Why? Well, paddlers standing on paddleboards have a higher center of gravity, making them more likely to fall off their boards.
- Never attempt to feed the alligators.

***Other Paddling Trails Nearby*** If you want to visit another paddling trail nearby, try the Buffalo Bayou Paddling Trail in downtown Houston, approximately 30 miles north, or the Galveston Island State Park Paddling Trail located on Galveston Island.

Buffalo Bayou Paddling Trail is the longest continuous paddling trail in the state at 26 miles. The trail starts near Highway 6 on the west side of Houston and winds through Houston, ending at Allen's Landing Park. Along the way, it passes through several parks, a greenway corridor, and wooded areas; it ends next to large skyscrapers downtown. If you choose to paddle the trail, you don't have to paddle the entire length because there are eight intermediate access points along the trail.

Galveston Island State Park Paddling Trail—Located south of Armand Bayou on Galveston Island is another paddling Trail. The trail is located on the 2,000-acre Galveston Island State Park. There are actually three trails that range in length from 2.6 to 4.8 miles. Each trail follows the shoreline and winds through the marsh. Hurricane Ike devastated the park and the paddling trail in 2008, but an aggressive state program, with help from volunteers, enabled work to begin to rebuild the park. The park has many amenities: a beach area, cabins and tent camping, boardwalks, and of course the paddling trail.

***Wildlife*** Because I have spent many hours on the water and paddled thousands of miles over the past thirty years, I have experienced a few unpredictable and extraordinary encounters with wildlife. Back in the 1990s, I once saw a white pelican near Tom Miller Dam in Austin. I knew that the coast was at least 115 miles away, as the pelican flies, and I had never seen a pelican anywhere in central Texas, but there it was, floating on the water just below the dam. When I paddled near, the pelican flew away with no apparent injury. More recently, in February 2015, I was paddling on the Colorado River approximately 2 miles upstream of the Columbus Paddling Trail. I was paddling my C-1 and my wife was paddling with a friend, Teddy Gray, some distance behind. As I passed under the Highway 71 bridge, I saw four large white birds several hundred yards upstream. While I could not identify the birds in the distance, I was puzzled because they were larger than great egrets, and I did not expect to see any swans in the area. When I paddled closer, I recognized the large, pink, floppy lower bill of a white pelican. The next weekend, I returned and to my surprise there were thirty-one white pelicans in the same area.

I will never forget the time I was paddling the Galveston Island State Park Paddling Trail. I was employed by Texas Parks and Wildlife Department and was responsible for managing the coastal paddling trails. I was replacing some of the numbered trail signs that were missing or in bad condition on the Dana Cove Loop Trail. Near the geo-textile breakwaters, I noticed a bird perched up ahead on one of the power-line poles. When I first saw it, I was confused because it looked like a cormorant, but it was much larger than the average cormorant. When I was about 30 yards away, the bird took off, and I immediately recognized the long slender wings of a magnificent frigate bird. Frigate birds have extremely long, pointed wings that reach 7½ feet in length. Males have a large gular pouch that, when inflated, looks like a red balloon. I had seen the birds while paddling the Sea of Cortez near the Baja Peninsula, in Mexico, but I had never seen one in Texas waters before.

On December 11, 2010, I was fishing just off the jetties near Port O'Connor. There were four in our party and it was a beautiful day. The sun was overhead and it had just begun to warm up. We had plenty of blue crab for bait and were excited about the possibility of catching a red drum or two. We were less than a mile from Fisherman's Cut and trail marker #1 of the Port O'Connor Paddling Trail. We had landed a few reds, but it was a bit slow, as fishing goes.

I had my bait overboard and was waiting for that familiar tug of a bull red. As I looked back toward Port O'Connor, I saw something in the water about 50 feet away. I was puzzled by the brown color and size and shape of the object. It was not a porpoise or a shark, in fact, it did not look like any fish I could identify. As it surfaced, I could not believe my eyes. I think I yelled out to everyone, and we all looked in amazement as the creature surfaced, took a quick gulp of air, and then dove down into the water. In amazement, we all looked at each other and were puzzled by what we had just seen. Then only a short distance away, the creature surfaced and I got a second look. Without a doubt, we all agreed, it was a manatee! Yes, that's right, a manatee.

# 9 Conservation Is Everyone's Job

Our rivers, streams, and other natural resources face major threats, such as an ever-increasing human population, habitat destruction, perturbations to water resources, exotic invasive species, and natural disasters.

## Human Population Growth

Texas, like all other states, has a set land area, but its population continues to grow. According to the US Census Bureau, Texas was the second-fastest-growing state from 2010 to 2015, and only California had more people than Texas. The "Water for Texas 2012 State Water Plan" states, "The Population in Texas is expected to increase significantly between 2010 and 2060, growing from 25.4 million to 46.3 million people."[1] That's an 82 percent increase. While rapid growth is good for the economy and vitality of Texas, it also presents many major environmental challenges for the future.

## Habitat Destruction

Since the first Texas settlers established colonies in the late 1600s, the landscape has completely changed. For example, more than half of the wetland habitat has been lost in the contiguous United States since European settlement began.[2] Small walking paths and dirt roads have been replaced by concrete and asphalt superhighways. Small one-street towns with wooden buildings have become large cities with steel, concrete, and glass skyscrapers. Small farms tilled by horse-drawn plows have been replaced by large commercial farms with tractors, combines, and other mechanized farm equipment. While all these improvements are the result of our modern lifestyle, major impacts to native wildlife have resulted. While some species can coexist, others have been extirpated when their essential habitat was modified or converted to a different land use.

Of the sixteen million acres of bottomland hardwoods and riparian habitat that existed in early Texas, more than 60 percent have been lost to agriculture, urban and industrial development, timber production, and reservoir construction. An original 1.2 million acres of coastal wetlands, so important to many aquatic species, has been reduced by 50 percent. Vast tallgrass prairies that once covered more than twenty million acres, have been drastically reduced. The original 12.6-million-acre Blackland Prairie has been reduced to a mere 100,000 acres of native sod.[3]

While impacts to the landscape are visible and obvious, impacts to subsurface water are not as apparent. Overpumping of groundwater for irrigation and human use has lowered groundwater tables and dried up springs. According to Gunnar Brune, of the 281 major springs that once existed in Texas, sixty-five no longer exist. Also, only seventeen of the original thirty-one large springs are still flowing. Future impacts are anticipated as increased groundwater pumping continues.[4]

## Water Resources

Over 191,000 miles of rivers and streams, seven major estuaries, over one thousand public reservoirs, and thousands of springs in Texas provide habitat for hundreds of aquatic species. With over 150 species of native freshwater fishes, Texas ranks among the most biologically diverse states. The future of these abundant aquatic resources depends largely upon many factors. Human influence on aquatic environments can degrade habitats. The importance and function of our rivers and streams is not always understood, and in some cases this lack of knowledge leads to bigger problems when people attempt to change their free-flowing nature. The need to understand the role and function of our rivers and streams, and communicate it to others, is the key to the conservation of healthy resources that can be enjoyed by present and future generations of Texans.

Wise use of our precious aquatic resources is important, and unless we are good stewards, these resources can be lost forever. Rivers supply nutrient-rich fresh water to coastal waters, and without these inflows, the vitality of the coastal waters can be significantly degraded. Some Texas rivers have been diverted and large reservoirs have been constructed that have disrupted the rivers' natural flow. Beginning in the late 1960s, state and federal laws were enacted to conserve important aquatic resources. However, approximately 150 major reservoirs had already been built before these laws were enacted that required mitigation for wildlife habitat lost to inundation. Another factor that affects our streams is water withdrawals for municipal, agricultural, and industrial uses. While water-rights permits issued by the Texas Commission on Environmental Quality (TCEQ) today include special conditions to protect downstream aquatic resources, most water-rights permits were issued before these special conditions were required. In addition, some river basins in Texas have very little water available for new water-rights permits.

> In general, Texas has very little water remaining, for appropriation to new users. In some river basins, water is over appropriated, meaning that the water rights already in place amount to more water than is typically available during drought.[5]

Which means that if all the permit holders were allowed to draw water during drought conditions, the river would dry up.

While only a quart of water, or so, is needed for each individual to maintain bodily functions, much more water is needed for each individual to carry on their daily lives. Water is needed for cooking, growing crops, ranching, manufacturing, and other human processes. According to the "Water for Texas 2012 State Water Plan," by 2060 the demand for water is expected to increase by 22 percent, but current supplies are expected to decrease from the current eighteen million acre-feet to 15.3 million acre-feet due primarily to the depletion of the Ogallala Aquifer.[6] Since future water needs are greater than dependable water sources, resource managers will face major challenges. Some strategies to provide more water supply include new reservoir construction, weather modification, conjunctive use of surface water and groundwater, aquifer storage and recovery, desalination, brush control, and rainwater management. Fortunately, water conservation and wastewater reuse will also help address Texas' future water needs.

Until the 1960s and '70s there was little concern for water pollution in Texas rivers.[7] By that time, significant environmental damage had already occurred, and the environment had paid a high price for economic growth. Some rivers had become devoid of fish, and others were unsafe to swim in. Large concentrations of chemicals were washed off the land by storm-water runoff. These pollutants were known as "nonpoint sources." While the current water permitting process provides better protection for extant aquatic resources, Texas still ranks among the leaders in pounds of pollutants discharged in Texas waters. Texas dumped 14.6 million pounds of industrial pollutants and toxic chemicals into Texas waterways in 2010 (Smith, 2013).[8] Only Indiana, Virginia, and Nebraska discharge more industrial pollutants.

## Invasive Species

The introduction of plant or animal species to North America began with European immigrants more than five hundred years ago.[9] Although some introductions were accidental, others were planned, and while well meaning, they posed significant adverse impacts upon the native flora and fauna. Sometimes called, "exotic," "alien," or "nonindigenous," these species often become invasive, causing new threats and ecological consequences. You may be familiar with nutria, English sparrows, cattle egrets, or other "exotic species." For the most part, these species are a nuisance, but they are not a major environmental problem. However, others pose an insurmountable problem that is out of control. These species cause major economic and environmental damages.

### Water Hyacinth

In 1884 at the World's Fair in New Orleans, a group of Japanese visitors brought a gift of beautiful aquatic plants with lush green leaves and lavender flowers. While it is not known how the plants reached the state's waters, within a few years water hyacinth (fig. 9.1) choked rivers, killed fish, and stopped shipping in Louisiana streams. After numerous attempts to control the plant, a grand scheme was proposed in 1910 to get rid of the plant. The plan was to import hippopotamuses from Africa to eat the hyacinth. The hippos would also be eaten to solve a meat shortage in the United States.

**FIGURE 9.1.** Water hyacinth

That same year, Louisiana Congressman Robert Broussard introduced the Hippo bill (H.R. 23621) in the US House of Representatives. While the bill apparently received some serious consideration, in the end, it failed by only one vote.

Water hyacinth is native to the Amazon Basin of South America, but it has been introduced to Asia, Australia, Africa, and other areas, where it has become a very noxious invasive plant. Water hyacinth is widespread in Texas waters, and in 2013 the plant was found in thirty-five public waters and covered 13,000 acres. In 2008, low flow in the Guadalupe River allowed a large raft of floating hyacinth to clog a section of the river downstream of Tivoli. In mid-June paddlers racing in the Texas Water Safari reported large rafts of hyacinth so thick that they had to pole their way through the plants. The raft of plants clogged the entire river for approximately 200 yards. Because the plant floats on top of the water, it can block light infiltration, affecting other plants, fish, and other aquatic life. Water hyacinth is one of more dreaded exotic invasive plants.

As mentioned in chapter 8, water hyacinth has choked sections of the Armand Bayou Paddling Trail. Major concentrations of the plant stack up in small coves and sheltered pockets of the bayou. In 2015, the Armand Bayou Nature Center hired a contractor to spray the plant. Hopefully, the spraying will control the plant, and flow in the stream will keep the plant from blocking the bayou.

## Hydrilla

Sometime in the 1950s Hydrilla (fig. 9.2) was introduced in the United States. Reportedly, Hydrilla was introduced into Florida from Sri Lanka via the aquarium trade, and the plants somehow ended up in Tampa Bay.[10] Within five years the plants spread throughout Florida and the southeastern United States.

I first witnessed an invasion of Hydrilla in the water-cooling pond at the Sam Seymour Power Plant near La Grange in Fayette County. The plant is coal-fired with a cooling pond that dilutes heated water generated by the plant. Because the cooling pond maintained a warmer water temperature, Hydrilla grew rapidly throughout the year. The growth of Hydrilla in the lake had gotten so bad that small boat traffic was very difficult.

I was working for the Texas Parks and Wildlife Department at the time and I was invited along with some of my colleagues to witness a demonstration of an aquatic mowing machine used to control Hydrilla. Governor George W. Bush was at the event along with a large contingent of onlookers, including the press. While the mowing machine seemed to work well, given the amount of Hydrilla in the pond, the machine could not eradicate the plant but could only be used to

**FIGURE 9.2.** Hydrilla

keep the boating lanes clear. Through the years Hydrilla has continued to spread to numerous Texas lakes, causing problems for resource managers. While eradication of the plant seems hopeless, and resource managers work diligently to contain it, the plant continues to be a biological and economic nightmare.

## Giant Salvinia

Giant Salvinia is, in my opinion, the most invasive and destructive exotic plant that has invaded Texas waters. The plant was first reported in 1998 in the Houston area and also in Toledo Bend Reservoir. Since then, it has been reported in Lake Conroe, Wright Patman Lake, Lake of the Pines, and more than twenty public waters. Like water hyacinth, the plant is native to the Amazon Basin of South America. Also, like hyacinth, it is a floating plant that blocks sunlight and decreases oxygen levels in the water. Thick concentrations of Salvinia, more than 2 feet thick, outgrow and replace native plants. As mentioned in chapter 8, giant Salvinia has covered large areas of Caddo Lake and continues to be a major obstruction to boat traffic in the lake.

## Zebra Mussel

One of the more recent invasive species reported in Texas waters is the zebra mussel. Zebra mussels are mollusks native to Russia. The first occurrence of the mussel was reported in Lake Texoma in 2009. Adults are only 1 ½ inches long and have distinctive dark stripes on their shell. The species is reportedly one of the most destructive and can adhere to almost any surface, including boats, boat trailers, dinghies, pipes, and buoys. Larval mussels are not visible to the naked eye and therefore can be transported from one lake to another in bait buckets or motorboat wells. Zebra mussels can cause declines in native mussels and other aquatic species by absorbing phytoplankton. They also increase light penetration and raise water temperatures. Large clusters of mussels have even sunk buoys. Since their discovery in 2009, they have been reported in the Red, Trinity, and Brazos Basins. The known distribution (as of July 27, 2015) of zebra mussels in Texas reservoirs was: Texoma, Ray Roberts, Lewisville, Bridgeport, Lavon, Waco, and Belton Lakes. Zebra mussels have also been found on isolated occasions in the Red River below Texoma, the Elm Fork of the Trinity River below Lake Ray Roberts, Sister Grove Creek above Lake Lavon, and a boat with zebra mussels attached was found in Lake Ray Hubbard. Transporting zebra mussels is illegal. To prevent their transport, recreational boaters should clean, drain, and dry their boats and equipment when moving from water body to water body. Experts say that in the future, zebra mussels have the potential to become the most destructive invasive species; technology is not currently available to eradicate them.

On rare occasions, exotic introductions can provide benefits that are well received by resource managers. For example, the Chinese ring-necked pheasant is an exotic game bird that is native to Asia. The introduction of the pheasant in the United States is an interesting story.

In 1877, United States Consul General Owen Denny and his wife Gertrude were stationed in Tientsin, China. After three years there, they were relocated to Shanghai. Impressed by the beautiful exotic birds and plants, the Dennys decided to ship several species home to Oregon. In January 1881, the Dennys loaded sixty Chinese ring-necked pheasants, several Mongolian sand grouse, and several tree species, including bamboo, on a ship bound for the United States. Two months later the ship arrived in Port Townsend, Oregon. Weathered, battered, and bruised, most of the pheasants survived the trip and were released on Sauvie Island in the Columbia River near Portland. From this small release, the Chinese ringed-necked pheasant established viable populations that spread to nineteen Rocky Mountain, Midwest, and Plains states and Canada. The ringed-necked pheasant is a popular game bird in Texas as well. The introduction of the ringed-necked pheasant has provided many hours of pleasure for those who enjoy the birds' beautiful plumage (fig. 9.3). They are also popular with hunters who travel to North Texas, where the birds are found.

**FIGURE 9.3.** Ring-necked pheasant

## Natural Disasters

Natural disasters such as hurricanes and tornados can devastate the landscape. Long-term drought can dry up rivers and lakes and threaten water and food supplies. Wildfires devastate everything in their path, and flood events damage homes and other structures near our rivers.

During the last several years (2010–15), low rainfall greatly affected the state's lakes and streams. By all accounts, the state was in a drought of historic proportions, with 2011 being the single driest year on record. This was particularly true in the central and western part of the state. Lake Travis, a water-supply lake near my home in Austin, remained almost 50 feet below conservation level for a two-year period between 2013 and 2014.

In 2011, drought conditions, strong winds, warm temperatures, and low humidity gave rise to a rash of wildfires in Texas. During that year, more than 31,000 fires burned more than 4,000,000 acres and nearly 3,000 homes. The most severe fire, and the most destructive wildfire in Texas history, began on September 4, 2011. Three separate fires, fueled by Tropical Storm Lee, merged into one blaze that burned for almost seven weeks. It destroyed 1,673 homes, thousands of acres of private land, the majority of the lands in Bastrop State Park, a portion of the unique Lost Pines Forest, and, sadly, two firefighters lost their lives.

With more than 367 miles of coastline, Texas is vulnerable to hurricanes that hit the Gulf Coast. According to the National Weather Service, Weather Prediction Center, from 1980 to the present, at least seventy tropical or subtropical hurricanes affected the state of Texas. Hurricane Ike in 2008 was the most severe hurricane in terms of damages and fatalities. The storm made landfall at Galveston, causing twelve billion dollars of damage in Texas and eighty-four deaths. The damage to Galveston was so severe that the town was declared uninhabitable after the storm. I visited Galveston Island State Park a few weeks after the storm and the entire park was in shambles. Debris was everywhere, park buildings were destroyed, and boats were sitting on dry land. I went down to check on the paddling trail. It was no longer there.

In summary, I suppose I may have painted a rather dismal picture of the future of our state's streams, lakes, and other natural resources. When I look around, I see litter cluttering our stream banks and highways. Unfortunately, we have become a throwaway society, and until this becomes unacceptable, things won't change. However, I am hopeful that the state's regulatory agencies will use their mandated authority to conserve Texas' diminishing natural resources.

There is, however, one statewide planning effort that gives me some optimism. In 2007, the Texas legislature passed Senate Bill 3. The legislation set up a statewide planning process to set environmental flow standards for new water-rights permits. The legislation established eleven regions of the state and a Stakeholder Committee for each. Additionally, an Expert Science Team was appointed by each Stakeholder Committee. Both the Science Committee and the Stakeholder Committee have made environmental flow recommendations to TCEQ, and TCEQ has adapted environmental flow standards for many basins in Texas. These environmental flow standards ensure that when new water rights are granted, an amount of water remains in the stream. This benefits the environment while balancing human needs. While the planning process is not complete, time will tell if this effort benefits aquatic resources.

While it is true that we face some major challenges, I think that there is strength in numbers. If we work together we can make a difference. You may be wondering, "What can I do to help conserve the state's natural resources?" That's a good question. I think that the first step is to get involved. How? As the familiar slogan goes, "Think globally and act locally." Be aware of what is happening around you and look for opportunities to get involved and make a difference.

You may want to join a conservation organization like the Audubon Society and learn more about the conservation of birds. You could join the Nature Conservancy and get involved in projects in your area. Become a volunteer in a state or federal conservation organization or become a Master Naturalist with Texas Parks and Wildlife Department and share your knowledge with others. You could create habitat for wildlife in your own backyard or convert it to a xeriscape. Replace fixtures in your house with those that conserve water and energy or plant a tree in the burned-out area of Bastrop State Park. Join a local paddling club and volunteer to clean up a section of a river or lake. Each year in March, a group of volunteers gets together and cleans up the entire 80 miles of the San Marcos River. You could contact the Meadows Center at Texas State University in San Marcos and join the "Texas Stream Team" and volunteer to monitor a local stream. You could attend a public hearing at TCEQ or a regional water planning meeting to learn more about water projects in your area. As a citizen, you have the right to have your voice heard. You can start a recycling program in your area for paper, plastic, and aluminum cans, or join the Texas Department of Transportation's Adopt a Highway Program and clean up a section of a highway right-of-way. You may think that one individual cannot make a difference; that's not true. I am reminded of one aquatic system in Central Texas, where individuals have made a significant difference.

## San Marcos Springs and River

Approximately 40 miles from my home in Austin is the town of San Marcos, and tucked neatly within the city limits are the San Marcos Springs. Flowing up from the limestone substrate, the spring complex provides a continuous flow of crystal clear water that runs downstream, forming the 80-mile San Marcos River (fig. 9.4). Known as one of the oldest, continually inhabited sites in North America, the springs and river have provided a dependable water source for thousands of years.[11] The San Marcos Springs were a gathering place for Native Americans dating back to somewhere around 9200 BC, and according to Jim Garber, an anthropologist at Texas State University, the springs were probably a place of religious significance.[12]

Since the original settlements, the springs have been altered by engineering and urban growth. The sensitive nature of the springs and river, the urban growth of the city, and the unparalleled attraction to recreational users, have made the area a center of controversy over the years.

In the 1950s, The Aquarena Springs theme park was located at the springs and offered an underwater submarine theater, a mermaid show, a swimming pig named Ralph, and glass-bottomed boat tours. The theme park operated until 1994, when Southwest Texas State University (now Texas State Univer-

**FIGURE 9.4.** The San Marcos River looking downstream from the headwaters at Spring Lake

sity) purchased the site.[13] Today, the site is the home of the Meadows Center for Water and the Environment at Texas State University, which conducts extensive research and educational programs on water resources in Texas and throughout the nation.

Over the years, pollution from urban growth and the San Marcos wastewater treatment plant, low water flows from outdated water usage laws, and wear and tear from recreation, have impacted the springs and river.

I will never forget the first time I saw the springs. I was a college student on a field trip to the area in the 1960s, and I remember reaching down into the vegetation near the hotel and pulling up aquatic plants with several San Marcos salamanders embedded in the vegetation. In 1980, the species was listed as "threatened" by the US Fish and Wildlife Service. Over the past thirty-five years, I have paddled the river on hundreds of occasions and worked on several projects on the river while employed by the Texas Parks and Wildlife Department.

During this time, I first met Tom Goynes, an expert canoeist, family man, part-time preacher, and last but not least full-time river advocate. Tom owned a canoe livery and campgrounds on the banks of the river. I bought my first boat, a kayak, from him in 1980, and over the next thirty-five years, I witnessed Tom's never-ending battle to protect the San Marcos River. Tom's name is synonymous with the San Marcos River. Whether he is organizing the annual cleanup of the entire river, testifying before the legislature in support of river conservation, heading up the Texas River Protection Association, or working to create a state recreation district to monitor and regulate recreational use and tubing on the river, no single individual has done more to conserve this river than Tom Goynes.

Also working to conserve the springs is a volunteer-based, nonprofit organization called the San Marcos River Foundation (SMRF). Created in 1985, SMRF has worked diligently to preserve and conserve the springs and river. While the acronym SMRF may give visions of a cartoon character, the small volunteer nonprofit is a major player in the conservation of the San Marcos Springs and River. In fact, the nonprofit foundation has done more to protect this precious resource than any other private organization or governmental entity. One of the cofounders, Dianne Wassenich, and I met in the 1980s and became better acquainted when she was on the Texas Parks and Wildlife Department's River Conservation Advisory Board. After seventeen years as a volunteer with SMRF, Dianne is now the program manager; I had a chance to sit down with her in June 2016 to discuss the organization's current work.

When I asked Dianne to identify the foundation's most significant accomplishments, she was quick to identify the city of San Marcos's new, improved, wastewater treatment plant. Back in the 1990s, the city tried to renew their permit for an aging wastewater treatment plant. Because the discharges from the plant did not provide adequate treatment for phosphorous, the plant posed a threat to the river's water quality. SMRF fought the city, requesting a discharge system that not only removed phosphorous and other pollutants but also improved the dissolved oxygen level. After a contentious hearing before the Texas Natural Resource Conservation Commission, the city decided to build a new, state-of-the-art plant that would greatly improve the quality of discharge into the river.

In 2000, SMRF took on another significant project when they boldly requested a water right to maintain flows in the San Marcos River. The action was unique because unlike other water-rights permits that withdraw water, the permit requested a water right to keep 1.15 million acre-feet of water in the river, which was the amount needed to maintain the river, according to the state's own study.

Over the next ten years the permit moved slowly through the administrative and legal processes. In the end, SMRF sued the Texas Natural Resource Conservation Commission; the district court ruled in favor of SMRF, but the state legislature passed legislation prohibiting an instream permit. While the permit was denied, this case accomplished another significant action. Because the permit process had gained national attention, American Rivers, a nationwide conservation organization, declared the Guadalupe and San Marcos Rivers as one of the Top Ten Endangered Rivers in 2003. This gave the river nationwide exposure.

Individuals can make a difference in their communities, whether it's by volunteering with local foundations and associations, like SMRF, assisting in citizen science surveys of endangered wild rice, or assisting in local river cleanups and removing invasive water hyacinth and elephant ears from the banks of the springs.

## Nashua River

I am reminded of a true story of a conservation effort that started with one person and ended up a statewide effort. Some years ago, I met Lynne Cherry, an author of wonderful children's books. Ms. Cherry came to Texas to research a book she was writing, and I drove her around. While on the road, she told me about a book she had written about a lady named Marion Stoddart who led a successful effort to clean up a polluted river.

In 1962 Marion Stoddart moved to Groton, Massachusetts. Near her home, the 37-mile Nashua River flowed northeast from Massachusetts and emptied into the Merrimack River near Nashua, New Hampshire. At that time, there were no laws regulating the discharge of waste into rivers and streams, and the Nashua River was one of the ten worst polluted rivers in the country. Reportedly, residents could smell the stench of the river a mile away.

Located along the banks of the river were paper mills that discharged dye and effluents into the river. On a given day, the water was colored green or red, or whatever the color the plants were discharging that day (fig. 9.5). Determined to clean up the river, Ms. Stoddart began a grassroots effort and made it her life's mission. Over the next few years, she began to spread the word and enlist thousands of citizens. Ms. Stoddart had no real experience in lobbying for a cause, but in her efforts, she left no stones unturned. She met with local elected officials and talked with industry executives whose enterprises were located along the river. She even sent a bottle of the smelly Nashua River water to Massachusetts governor John Volpe; she also sent a petition signed by over 6,200 citizens protesting the condition of the river. After four years of hard work, her efforts

**FIGURE 9.5.** Nashua River before cleanup in the 1960s.
Courtesy of Nashua River Watershed Association

payed off when the Massachusetts legislature passed the Massachusetts Clean Water Act of 1966. The act provided funding to construct wastewater treatment plants in the area. Four years later treatment plants were completed and became operational.

Today the Nashua River Watershed Association, which was founded by Marion Stoddart, continues the work that she started. The river has recovered, and in fact, in 2014, Congress passed a bill that authorized a study to include portions of the Nashua River as a Wild and Scenic River (fig. 9.6). Wouldn't it be a fitting ending to this story if one of the nation's ten most polluted rivers became a Wild and Scenic River?

I had the pleasure of meeting Marion Stoddart in 1996. It was at the Annual Meeting of the United States Canoe Association in Lisle, Illinois. Ms. Stoddart was the recipient of the Mike Freemont Conservation Award. The award was given to Ms. Stoddart for her conservation work on the Nashua River.

**FIGURE 9.6.** Nashua River today.
Courtesy of Nashua River Watershed Association

# Appendix 1

## *Suggested List of Canoe Gear*

Personal flotation device (PFD)
One paddle for each paddler and an extra one (in case you drop or break one)
Waterproof bag or hard container
Sponge or bailer
Water and snack food
Rain gear
Painter tied to the bow and stern
A headlamp or flashlight and whistle
Change of clothes (quick dry clothing is recommended because wet cotton is a poor insulator)
Hat or cap
Sunshades
Comfortable water shoes or running shoes
First aid kit
Cell phone
Sunscreen
Lanyards
GPS or map
Throw line

**Overnight or multiday trip, add the following equipment:**

Tent
Sleeping bag
Extra clothes
Sleeping pad
Cook stove and fuel
Plate or bowl, cup, and eating utensils
Food and water for the number of days planned
Toilet paper
Matches or fire starter

# Appendix 2

## *Wildlife Observed on the Paddling Trails*

### Birds

American avocet
American coot
American crow
American oystercatcher
American robin
anhinga
bald eagle
belted kingfisher
black-crowned night heron
black-necked stilt
black skimmer
black vulture
blue-winged teal
boat-tailed grackle
brown pelican
bufflehead
canvasback
cardinal
caracara
Caspian tern
cattle egret
cliff swallow
common crow
common gallinule
common goldeneye
common grackle
common tern
double-crested cormorant
great blue heron
great egret
green heron
green kingfisher
green-winged teal
Harris's hawk
killdeer
laughing gull
lesser scaup
little blue heron
long-billed curlew
Louisiana heron
magnificent frigatebird
mallard
mourning dove
mute swan
northern shoveler
osprey
peregrine falcon
pied-billed grebe
pileated woodpecker
piping plover
reddish egret
red-headed woodpecker
red-shouldered hawk
red-tailed hawk
red-winged blackbird
Rio Grande turkey
roadrunner
rock dove
roseate spoonbill
scissor-tailed flycatcher
snow goose
snowy egret
spotted sandpiper
turkey vulture
white-fronted goose
white ibis
white pelican
white-winged dove
willet
wood duck
wood stork
yellow-crowned night heron

## Mammals

armadillo
axis deer
beaver
cottontail rabbit
eastern fox squirrel
eastern gray squirrel
feral hog
manatee
Mexican free-tailed bat
mink
nutria
raccoon
rock squirrel
swamp rabbit
white-tailed deer

## Reptiles

American alligator
common snapping turtle
red-eared turtle
Texas slider

## Amphibians

bull frog

## Fish

largemouth bass
red drum
speckled trout

# Appendix 3

## *List of State Paddling Trails*

| # | Trail Name | Travel and Tourism Regions | Nearby Towns | Water Body | Length Miles | LAT (WGS 84) | LONG (WGS 84) |
|---|---|---|---|---|---|---|---|
| 1 | Buffalo Bayou | Gulf Coast | Houston | Buffalo Bayou | 26.0 | 29.76937500 | -95.66002833 |
| 2 | South Bay | Gulf Coast | S. Padre Island | South Bay | 8.0 | 26.04862000 | -97.18147000 |
| 3 | Christmas Bay | Gulf Coast | Galveston | Christmas Bay | 19.1 | 29.04890000 | -95.16562000 |
| 4 | Lighthouse Lakes | Gulf Coast | Aransas Pass | Redfish Bay | — | 27.86216 | -97.07589 |
| | Cutter Loop | Gulf Coast | Aransas Pass | Redfish Bay | 5.0 | | |
| | South Bay Loop | Gulf Coast | Aransas Pass | Redfish Bay | 6.7 | | |
| | Redfish Loop | Gulf Coast | Aransas Pass | Redfish Bay | 6.8 | | |
| | Electric Lake Loop | Gulf Coast | Aransas Pass | Redfish Bay | 1.25 | | |
| 5 | Armand Bayou | Gulf Coast | Clear Lake | Armand Bayou | 8.2 | 29.58827 | -95.07018 |
| 6 | Galveston Island | Gulf Coast | Galveston | Galveston Bay | — | 29.21472222 | -94.95388889 |
| | Dana Cove | Gulf Coast | Galveston | Galveston Bay | 2.4 | | |
| | Oak Bayou | Gulf Coast | Galveston | Galveston Bay | 4.8 | | |
| | Jenkin Bayou | Gulf Coast | Galveston | Galveston Bay | 2.8 | | |
| 7 | Mustang Island | Gulf Coast | Port Aransas | Corpus Christi Bay | — | 27.73744000 | -97.13750000 |
| | Shamrock Loop | Gulf Coast | Port Aransas | Corpus Christi Bay | 5.2 | | |
| | North Trail | Gulf Coast | Port Aransas | Corpus Christi Bay | 8.5 | | |
| | Ashum Trail | Gulf Coast | Port Aransas | Corpus Christi Bay | 6.8 | | |
| 8 | Port O'Connor | Gulf Coast | Port O'Connor | Espirito Santo Bay | — | 28.43863333 | -96.41401667 |
| | Matagorda Island | Gulf Coast | Port O'Connor | Espirito Santo Bay | 25.0 | | |
| | Pass Cavallo / J-Hook | Gulf Coast | Port O'Connor | Espirito Santo Bay | 11.0 | | |
| | Barron Bay | Gulf Coast | Port O'Connor | Espirito Santo Bay | 8.0 | | |

| # | Trail Name | Travel and Tourism Regions | Nearby Towns | Water Body | Length Miles | LAT (WGS 84) | LONG (WGS 84) |
|---|---|---|---|---|---|---|---|
| | Mules Slough | Gulf Coast | Port O'Connor | Espirito Santo Bay | 13.0 | | |
| | Fish Pond | Gulf Coast | Port O'Connor | Espirito Santo Bay | 16.0 | | |
| | Big Pocket | Gulf Coast | Port O'Connor | Espirito Santo Bay | 17.0 | | |
| 9 | Lady Bird Lake | Hill Country | Austin | Lady Bird Lake | — | 30.29111944 | -97.78785278 |
| | Tom Miller Dam Loop | Hill Country | Austin | Lady Bird Lake | 3.15 | | |
| | Barton Springs Loop | Hill Country | Austin | Lady Bird Lake | 3.25 | | |
| | Festival Beach Loop | Hill Country | Austin | Lady Bird Lake | 4.8 | | |
| 10 | Pecan Bayou | Hill Country | Brownwood | Pecan Bayou | 3.2, 4.0 | 31.779812 | -98.980476 |
| 11 | South Llano | Hill Country | Junction | South Llano River | 6.0 | 30.449800 | -99.812770 |
| 12 | Upper Guadalupe-Nichol's Landing | Hill Country | Spring Branch | Guadalupe River | 9.9 | 29.879416 | -98.448278 |
| 13 | Benton Lake | Pineywoods | Uncertain | Big Cypress Bayou | 2.4 | 32.71136 | -94.22906 |
| 14 | Clear Lake | Pineywoods | Uncertain | Big Cypress Bayou | 2.9 | 32.71136 | -94.22906 |
| 15 | Haggerty Creek | Pineywoods | Uncertain | Big Cypress Bayou | 5.0 | 32.71136 | -94.22906 |
| 16 | Mill Pond | Pineywoods | Uncertain | Big Cypress Bayou | 7.2 | 32.69200 | -94.18000 |
| 17 | Old River II | Pineywoods | Uncertain | Big Cypress Bayou | 3.0 | 32.71136 | -94.22906 |
| 18 | Carter's Chute | Pineywoods | Uncertain | Caddo Lake | 7.6 | 32.73919 | -94.16671 |
| 19 | Cathedral | Pineywoods | Uncertain | Caddo Lake | 3.8 | 32.71270 | -94.12024 |
| 20 | Hell's Half Acre | Pineywoods | Uncertain | Caddo Lake | 8.8 | 32.69382 | -94.17573 |
| 21 | Old Folks Playground | Pineywoods | Uncertain | Caddo Lake | 4.9 | 32.70242 | -94.12227 |
| 22 | Turtle Shell | Pineywoods | Uncertain | Caddo Lake | 4.6 | 32.70755 | -94.11843 |
| 23 | Cherokee Neches | Pineywoods | Jacksonville | Neches River | 6.6 | 31.94579 | -95.44468 |
| 24 | Cooks Lake to Scattermana | Pineywoods | Beaumont | Neches River/ Pine Isl Bayou | 4.8 | 30.15523 | -94.11588 |
| 25 | Neches | Pineywoods | Jasper | Neches River | 3.2 | 30.86292 | -94.18282 |
| 26 | Walnut Slough | Pineywoods | Jasper | B. A. Steinberger Lake | 4.3 | 30.86292 | -94.18282 |

| # | Trail Name | Travel and Tourism Regions | Nearby Towns | Water Body | Length Miles | LAT (WGS 84) | LONG (WGS 84) |
|---|---|---|---|---|---|---|---|
| 27 | Sandy Creek | Pineywoods | Jasper | B. A. Steinberger Lake | 4.9 | 30.84347 | -94.16662 |
| 28 | Bevilport | Pineywoods | Jasper | Angelina & Neches Rivers | 9.6, 12 | 30.92396667 | -94.16690833 |
| 29 | Mineola Big Foot | Pineywoods | Mineola | Sabine | 11.9 | 32.61296000 | -95.48605000 |
| 30 | Neches-Davey Crockett | Pineywoods | Lufkin | Neches River | 9.2 | 31.44460278 | -95.34170556 |
| 31 | Village Creek | Pineywoods | Silsbee | Village Creek | 21 | 30.397803 | -94.264656 |
| 32 | El Camino Real | Prairies and Lakes | Bastrop | Colorado River | 6.0 | 30.11194444 | -97.32497222 |
| 33 | Wilbarger | Prairies and Lakes | Bastrop | Colorado River | 14.3 | 30.16827778 | -97.40227778 |
| 34 | Beaver Pond | Prairies and Lakes | Denton | Lake Lewisville | 1 | 33.51442222 | -96.98149167 |
| 35 | Bosque Bluffs | Prairies and Lakes | Waco | Bosque River | 2.2 | 31.59290000 | -97.16929000 |
| 36 | Brazos Bridges | Prairies and Lakes | Waco | Brazos River | 4.8 | 31.59290000 | -97.16929000 |
| 37 | Bridgeport Falls | Prairies and Lakes | Bridgeport | Trinity River (West Fork) | 5.8 | 33.19574722 | -97.75591389 |
| 38 | Chupacabra Point | Prairies and Lakes | Runaway Bay | Lake Bridgeport | — | 33.15766000 | -97.87234000 |
|  | Boone Creek | Prairies and Lakes | Runaway Bay | Boone Creek | 4.0 |  |  |
|  | Willow Creek | Prairies and Lakes | Runaway Bay | Willow Creek | 4.0 |  |  |
|  | Cool Bed Creek | Prairies and Lakes | Runaway Bay | Cool Bed Creek | 4.0 |  |  |
| 39 | Columbus | Prairies and Lakes | Columbus | Colorado River | 6.5 | 29.71283333 | -96.54661111 |
| 40 | Dallas Trinity | Prairies and Lakes | Dallas | Trinity River (West Fork) | 10.2 | 32.78964444 | -96.84743333 |
| 41 | Fort Worth Nature Center | Prairies and Lakes | Fort Worth | Trinity River (West Fork) | 6.7 | 32.84835 | -97.47429 |
| 42 | Come and Take It | Prairies and Lakes | Gonzales | Guadalupe River | 11.0 | 29.47066100 | -97.48985800 |
| 43 | Independence | Prairies and Lakes | Gonzales | Guadalupe River | 2.6 | 29.28408000 | -97.44819400 |
| 44 | Guadalupe Valley | Prairies and Lakes | Cuero | Guadalupe River | 13.8 | 30.34711944 | -97.32789444 |
| 45 | Joe Pool | Prairies and Lakes | Grande Prairie | Joe Pool Lake/ Walnut Creek | 4.9 | 32.60684444 | -97.06313611 |

| # | Trail Name | Travel and Tourism Regions | Nearby Towns | Water Body | Length Miles | LAT (WGS 84) | LONG (WGS 84) |
|---|---|---|---|---|---|---|---|
| 46 | Lake Arlington | Prairies and Lakes | Arlington | Lake Arlington | 10.9 | 32.71275000 | -97.20213889 |
| 47 | Limestone Bluffs | Prairies and Lakes | Mexia | Navasota River | 5.3 | 31.63333333 | -96.56194444 |
| 48 | Luling Zedler Mill | Prairies and Lakes | Luling | San Marcos River | 6.0 | 29.66790694 | -97.69991083 |
| 49 | Morgan's Point Resort | Prairies and Lakes | Temple | Belton Lake | 3.6, 4.7, 0.9 | 31.14425500 | -97.47283100 |
| 50 | Paddle Point Creek | Prairies and Lakes | Rowlett | Lake Ray Hubbard | 6.4 | 32.89226667 | -96.53690278 |
| 51 | River Legacy Parks | Prairies and Lakes | Arlington | Trinity River (West Fork) | 2.0–8.0 | 32.78820556 | -97.10033333 |
| 52 | Goliad | South Texas Plains | Goliad | San Antonio River | 6.6 | 28.65252778 | -97.43138889 |
| 53 | Saspamco | South Texas Plains | San Antonio | San Antonio River | 12.0 | 29.22198000 | -98.35542700 |
| 54 | Seguin (Lake Seguin) | South Texas Plains | Seguin | Guadalupe River | 4.0 | 29.56123333 | -97.97179722 |
| 55 | Seguin (Lake Nolte/Meadow Lake) | South Texas Plains | Seguin | Guadalupe River | 2.6–8.4 | 29.55850000 | -97.96171000 |
| 56 | Victoria | South Texas Plains | Victoria | Guadalupe River | 25.0 | 28.89700000 | -97.13900000 |
| 57 | Columbia Bottomland | South Texas Plains | Angleton | Brazos River | 8.3 | 29.20102000 | -95.56423100 |
| 58 | Old Settlement Passage | Gulf Coast | West Columbia | Brazos River | 10.4 | 29.14076600 | -95.61534400 |
| 59 | Sugar Mill Stretch | Gulf Coast | Brazoria | Brazos River | 6.9 | 29.04811700 | -95.53414800 |
| 60 | Gulf Prairie Run | Gulf Coast | Lake Jackson | Brazos River | 9.8 | 29.03160400 | -95.47707000 |

# Appendix 4

## *List of National Organizations and Local Paddling Clubs*

### National Organizations

**1. American Canoe Association.** The organization was formed in the later part of the nineteenth century when a group of small boat enthusiasts gathered at Lake George in upper New York State. The year was 1880, and Nathaniel Holmes Bishop sent out an invitation to fellow canoeists to attend a canoe congress. Mr. Bishop was well known by other canoeists from his long canoe trips; he even took one long trip in a canoe made of paper. In response to his invitation, a small group of canoe enthusiasts met to share experiences and information. One outcome of the meeting was the creation of the American Canoe Association (ACA). One of the first orders of business was the establishment of five racing classes for canoes. Because canoe sailing was popular at that time, several classes included canoes with sails.

Since its creation, the ACA has continued to grow from a grassroots organization to a corporation that has influenced paddle sports across the United States. The ACA served as the national governing body for Olympic canoe and kayak racing from 1932 until 1987, when USA Canoe and Kayak (USACK) split off from the organization as a separate entity.

Today, the organization is involved in every aspect of recreational paddle sports, including instructor certification, waterway stewardship, safety, education, water trails, insurance for water-related events, and the publication of a bimonthly magazine, *Paddler*. A recent public announcement from USACK revealed that while it operated for many years as a separate entity, the organization plans to merge with the American Canoe Association, as one entity. Only time will tell if this becomes a reality. ACA's website is www.americancanoe.org.

**2. United States Canoe Association.** On January 6 and 7, 1968, a group of Midwest canoeists met at the Turkey Run Inn State Park in Indiana to discuss the creation of a new canoe racing organization. The group had petitioned the ACA to support canoe and kayak racing, but when their attempts were unsuccessful, they decided to form a new national organization, the United States Canoe Association (USCA). Over the years, the organization has continued to support and promote marathon canoe and kayak racing. While its principle interest is marathon canoe racing, the association also promotes and encourages canoe cruising, conservation, camping, and camaraderie. With a membership of only one thousand members or less, the volunteer organization continues to host an annual USCA National Canoe and Kayak Championship Race each August. The USCA also has a canoe instruction program and offers insurance for canoe races across the country.

Every two years the membership elects delegates from different regions of the country, and these delegates meet each January to conduct the business of the association. A volunteer executive committee is made up of an executive director, president, vice president, treasurer, and a secretary, which are all elected by the delegates. The association produces a quarterly magazine called *Canoe News*; their website is www.uscanoe.org.

**3. USA Canoe and Kayak.** USA Canoe and Kayak is the national governing body for competitive canoe and kayak racing in the United States. The nonprofit organization split from the ACA in 1987 and is currently responsible for coaching and sanctioning a team of athletes to compete in national and international canoe and kayak competitions. While their primary focus is to train and develop competitive canoe and kayak sprinters and whitewater paddlers, they also sanction other paddling sports, including marathon, canoe polo, outrigger canoe, dragon boat, canoe slalom, and stand-up paddle boarding. In 2015, the USACK and the ACA began to form a partnership, which included sharing of administrative staff. Recent reports by both USACK and ACA indicate that a possible merger of the two entities may be forthcoming. The website of USA Canoe and Kayak is www.teamusa.org/usa-canoe-kayak.

## Texas Clubs and Organizations

### Aggieland Paddle Club

College Station
http://www.race360.com/clubs/profile.asp?cid=34863

### Alamo City Rivermen

San Antonio
http://www.alamocityrivermen.org

### Austin Area Paddlers

Austin
https://www.meetup.com/AustinAreaPaddlers/

### Bayou City Whitewater Club

Houston
https://groups.yahoo.com/neo/groups/bcwc-1 /info

### Coastal Bend Paddlers Club

Victoria
Charlie Kouba, Charlie.kouba@classicnet.net
Coastal Bend Paddlers Club on Facebook

**Dallas Downriver Club**
Dallas
www.down-river.com

**East Texas Paddling Club**
http://www.facebook.com/EastTexasPaddlingClub
easttexaspaddlers@gmail.com
http://easttexaspaddlingclub.blogspot.com/

**Hill Country Paddlers Canoe Club**
Kerrville
http://www.race360.com/clubs/profile.asp?cid=34866

**Houston Association of Sea Kayakers**
Houston/Galveston
www.hask.org

**Houston Canoe Club**
Houston
(713) 467-8857
www.houstoncanoeclub.org

**Neches River Runners**
Palestine
903-723-2066
https://www.facebook.com/NechesRiverRunners

**North Texas River Runners**
Fort Worth
https://sites.google.com/a/river-runners.org/north-texas-river-runners/

**The Saturday Paddlers**
San Antonio
210-824-3237

**Texas Canoe and Kayak Racing Association**
tckra.org
Texas Canoe and Kayak Racing Association on Facebook

# Appendix 5

## *Suggested Readings on Texas Rivers*

1. *Paddling the Wild Neches*, Richard M. Donovan
2. *Living Waters of Texas*, Ken W. Kramer and Charles Kruvand
3. *San Marcos: A River's Story*, Jim Kimmel and Jerry Touchstone Kimmel
4. *Exploring the Brazos River: From Beginning to End*, Jim Kimmel and Jerry Touchstone Kimmel
5. *River of Contrasts: The Texas Colorado*, Margie Crisp
6. *Paddling the Guadalupe*, Wayne H. McAlister
7. *Canoeing and Kayaking Houston Waterways*, Natalie H. Wiest
8. *Running the River: Secrets of the Sabine*, Wes Ferguson and Jacob Craft Botter
9. *Neches River User Guide*, Gina Donovan
10. *Goodbye to a River*, John Graves
11. *Caddo: Visions of a Southern Cypress Lake*, Thad Sitton and photos by Carolyn Brown
12. *Rivers and Rapids*, Ben Nolan and Bob Naramore

# Notes

## Chapter 2

1. Jim Poling Sr., *The Canoe: An Illustrated History* (Woodstock, VT: Countryman Press, 2000), 14.

2. Ibid., 22.

3. Ibid., 31–34.

4. Ibid., 46.

5. Ibid., 62.

6. John Jennings, ed. *Bark Canoes* (Toronto: Firefly Books, 2012), 42–45.

7. Poling, *The Canoe*, 58.

8. Ibid., 62.

9. Ted Moores, "From Forest to Factory," in *The Canoe, A Living Tradition*, by John Jennings (Toronto: Firefly Books, 2002), 164.

10. Ibid., 160–78.

## Chapter 3

1. Steve Mitchell, "The Birth of Fiberglass Boats," *Good Old Boat* 2, no. 6 (1999): 23, 24.

2. Hallie Bond, "Paddling for Pleasure in the Northeastern States," in *The Canoe, A Living Tradition*, by John Jennings (Toronto: Firefly Books, 2002), 210.

3. Ibid.

4. Ibid.

5. Jason Gorss, *High Performance Carbon Fibers* (Washington, DC: American Chemical Society, 2003), 1.

## Chapter 7

1. Larry McKinney, "Water for the Future," *Outdoor Magazine of Texas*, July 2002, 23.

2. Thad Sitton, *Caddo: Visions of a Southern Cypress Lake* (College Station: Texas A&M University Press, 2015), 5–9.

3. Jim Poling Sr., *The Canoe: An Illustrated History* (Woodstock, VT: Countryman Press, 2000), 135.

4. Harte-Hanks Communications, Inc., "A Report by the Texas Poll," Austin, TX, July 1996, 1–14.

## Chapter 8

1. Merlin D. Tuttle, *Texas Bats* (Austin, TX: Bat Conservation International, 2003), 65–67.

2. Francis E. Abernethy, Handbook of Texas Online, "Big Thicket," Texas State Historic

Association, Austin, TX, 2010, 1–4. http://www.tshaonline.org/handbook/online/articles/gkb03.

3. National Parks Service, Big Thicket Preserve, www.nps.gov.

4. Ibid.

5. US Geological Survey, National Weather System, Gauge 08167500, 2011–16.

6. Thad Sitton and James Conrad, eds., *Every Sun That Rises: Wyatt Moore of Caddo Lake* (Austin: University of Texas Press, 1985), 11, 12.

7. Ibid.

8. Texas Parks and Wildlife Department, "Renovated Matagorda Island Lighthouse," news release, Austin, TX, May 17, 2004, 1.

9. Ricky L. Langley, "Alligator Attacks on Humans in the United States," *Wilderness and Environmental Medicine* 16 (2005): 118–24.

### Chapter 9

1. Texas Water Development Board, "Water for Texas 2012 State Water Plan," http://www.twdb.texas.gov/publications/state_water_plan/2012/2012_SWP.pdf.

2. Conservation Foundation, *Protecting America's Wetlands: An Action Agenda* (Waldorf, MA: Harper Graphics, 1988), 1.

3. Texas Parks and Wildlife Department, "Natural Agenda: A Strategic Plan for Texas Parks and Wildlife Department," Austin, TX, 1993.

4. Gunnar Brune, *Springs of Texas*, vol. 1. College Station: Texas A&M University Press, 2002). First published 1981.

5. Texas Water Development Board, "Water for Texas 2012 State Water Plan."

6. Ibid.

7. Lawrence E. Estaville and Richard A. Earl, *Texas Water Atlas* (College Station: Texas A&M University Press, 2008).

8. Sonia Smith, "Texas Waterways Are Nation's Fourth Most Polluted," *Texas Monthly*, January 21, 2013.

9. M. J. Mac, P. A. Opler, C. E. Puckett Haecker, and P. D. Doran, eds., *Status and Trends of the Nation's Biological Resources*, vols. 1 and 2 (Washington, DC: US Department of Interior, US Geological Survey, 1998).

10. D. C. Schmitz, B. V. Nelson, L. E. Nall, and J. D. Schardt, "Exotic Aquatic Plants in Florida: A Historical Perspective and Review of the Present Aquatic Plant Regulation Program," in "Proceedings of the Symposium on Exotic Pest Plants (Center, T. D., et al., eds.). Held on November 2–4, 1988, University of Miami, Rosentiel School of Martine and Atmospheric Science, Miami, Florida" (Washington, DC: US Department of the Interior, National Park Service Document, 1991), 303–23.

11. Dianne Wassenich, "Springing to Life," in *The Living Waters of Texas*, ed. Ken Kramer and Charles Kruvand (College Station: Texas A&M University Press, 2010), 31.

12. Clarisa Marcee, "Sacred Springs," *Outdoor Magazine of Texas*, June 1999, 22a.

13. Ibid., 23a.

# Glossary

**batten**. A long, flattened strip of wood or metal that is used to brace or support a boat

**bent-shaft paddle**. A type of canoe paddle with a blade attached to the shaft with a slight offset angle of 12 to 15 degrees

**blade**. The flattened portion of a paddle or oar that is attached to the shaft that pushes against the water when a stroke is made

**bow**. The front of the canoe

**bow seat**. The seat in the front of a tandem canoe

**C-1**. A canoe that holds only one paddler

**C-2**. A canoe that holds two paddlers

**capsize**. To turn a canoe on its side or upside down in the water

**carabiner**. A metal loop with a spring-loaded, hinged gate that is used to connect items together

**carbon fiber**. A lightweight material made of heated graphite that is used in the manufacture of canoes

**catch**. The beginning of a paddle stroke when the blade is inserted in the water and force is applied to the blade

**cavitate**. The unsteady movement and/or formation of bubbles created when the paddle is not pulled with a steady even force

**cockpit.** The portion of a decked canoe/kayak where the paddler sits

**composite**. The process of combining fibers and resin to create a composite material

**cygnet**. A young swan

**deck plate**. The upper part of the canoe, attached to the gunnels. Can be a small triangular piece at the bow or stern, or can cover a large part of the top area

**double blade paddle**. A kayak paddle that has a blade on each end of the staff

**draw stroke**. The stroke in which the blade of the paddle is placed out from the canoe and pulled toward the side

**Eskimo roll**. A method for righting a capsized kayak by using body motion and a paddle

**exit**. The end of a canoe stroke when the blade is removed from the water

**feathering**. The act of maneuvering the angle of a paddle blade to reduce air or water resistance

**fiberglass**. A type of reinforced plastic that is made of glass fibers

**foot brace**. A bar or brace in the bottom of a canoe where paddlers place their feet

**freeboard**. The portion of the canoe's hull that is above the waterline

**geocache**. An item or container that may contain other items, which is hidden and its GPS coordinates posted on the Internet for others to find

**GPS receiver**. A hand-held device used to locate geographic locations, time, and speed

**grip**. The very top of the paddle where the paddler places his or her hand

**gunwales**. The top of the hull in an open canoe

**gunnels**. The top of the hull in an open canoe

**heat exhaustion**. A condition of the body overheating, sometimes caused by an excessive loss of water and salt from sweating. Frequently due to exercising in a hot environment.

**hull**. The main body of the canoe

**hyperthermia**. Greatly elevated body temperature

**hyponatremia**. Abnormally low sodium (salt) in a person's blood. Can be a result of dehydration, drinking too much water, and excessive sweating and exercise.

**hypothermia**. A condition that exists when the human body loses heat faster than it can produce it

**keel**. A hard surface strip or structure on a canoe that runs down the bottom of the canoe from bow to stern; the structure adds strength to the hull and aids in tracking

**keel-line**. An imaginary line that runs from bow to stern that divides the canoe into equal part halves

**kevlar**. A lightweight material developed by the DuPont Company in 1965 that is bullet-proof and is used in the manufacture of canoes

**life jacket**. A jacket or vest that is lightweight and when worn by a person, aids in flotation. Life jackets are sanctioned and classified by the US Coast Guard

**lanyard**. A cord used around the neck or wrist to attach items: knife, flashlight, lip balm, and such

**neck**. The portion of paddle that joins the blade to the shaft

**oil can**. A visible flexing of a canoe hull that occurs when water pushes against it

**outrigger**. A type of ocean canoe that is paddled in rough water that has a stabilizing lateral float called an "outrigger" or "ama"

**paddle**. A linear device with a flattened end(s) used to propel a canoe or kayak through the water

**painter**. A rope or line that is attached to the bow and/or the stern of a canoe that aids in portages and launching and docking a canoe

**personal flotation device (PFD)**. See life jacket

**portage**. To exit a canoe from the water, carry across land, and put back into the water

**power face**. The side of the canoe blade that pushes against the water during a stroke

**power phase**. The portion of a canoe stroke when power is applied to the blade

**put-in**. A place to enter the water

**raptor**. A bird of prey

**recovery**. Part of the paddle stroke when the paddle returns from exiting the water to the catch

**resin**. Substance used with fiberglass, carbon fiber, and other materials, in combination with chemicals, that hardens to produce and/or repair boat hulls or paddles

**ribs**. Strips that run laterally from gunwale to gunwale that support the shape of the hull

**rocker**. The upward curve of the hull at the bow and stern of the canoe. The greater the curve, the easier to turn.

**Royalex**. A laminated material developed by the Uniroyal Company in 1960 that was used in the manufacture of recreational canoes and kayaks

**shaft**. The portion of a paddle that joints the blade to the grip

**shuttle**. The act of driving cars to or from the put-in or take-out

**single blade**. A canoe paddle

**solo canoe**. A canoe or kayak designed to carry one paddler

**stand-up paddleboard**. A flat watercraft that is paddled from a standing position

**stern**. The rear of the canoe

**take-out**. A point on the bank where you take the canoe out of the water

**throw bags**. A bag with a rope coiled inside that can be thrown to a canoe or paddler in trouble

**thwart**. The braces or supports that are attached to the canoe gunwales

**tracking**. The ability of a canoe to travel in a straight line

**trim**. A measure of the weight distribution in a canoe

**tumblehome**. The inward curve of the hull from its widest point near the waterline to the gunwales

**unlimited canoe**. A canoe or kayak that has no standard specifications

**wake**. A small wave that is created by a canoe when it moves through the water

**yoke**. A reinforced middle thwart that is used by one person to carry a canoe on his/her shoulders

## References and Literature Cited


Abernethy, Francis E. Handbook of Texas Online, "Big Thicket." Texas State Historic Association, Austin, TX, 2010. http://www.tshaonline.org/handbook/online/articles/gkb03.

Alvarez, Elizabeth Cruce, ed. Texas State Historical Association, Denton, TX, 2014.

American Red Cross. "Wilderness and Remote First Aid, Stay Well." Yardley, PA, 2010.

Bauer, Jack, Roy Frye, and Bob Spain. "A Natural Resource Survey for Proposed Reservoir Sites and Selected Stream Segments in Texas." Texas Parks and Wildlife Department, Austin, TX, 1991.

Beymer, Robert, and Louis Dzierzak. *Boundary Waters Canoe Area: Western Region*. Berkeley, CA: Wilderness Press, 2009.

Bond, Hallie. "Paddling for Pleasure in the Northeastern States." In *The Canoe, A Living Tradition*, by John Jennings, 194–211. Toronto: Firefly Books, 2002.

Brune, Gunnar. *Springs of Texas, vol. 1*. College Station: Texas A&M University Press, 2002. First published 1981.

Bull, John, and John Farrand Jr. *The Audubon Society Field Guide to North American Birds*. New York: Alfred A. Knopf, 1977.

Burt, William Henry, and Richard Philip Grossenheider. *A Field Guide to the Mammals*. Cambridge, MA: Riverside Press, 1964.

Conservation Foundation. *Protecting America's Wetlands: An Action Agenda*. Waldorf, MA: Harper Graphics, 1988.

D'Entremont, Jeremy. "Texas's 'Lydia Ann' Shines On." *Lighthouse Digest*, May 2007. http://www.lighthousedigest.com/Digest/StoryPage.cfm?StoryKey=2649.

Drost, Beth, "Grand Portage: The Great Carrying Place." National Parks Service, 2014.

Editors of Canoe and Kayak Magazine and Dennis O. Stuhaug. *The Complete Idiot's Guide to Canoeing and Kayaking*. El Segundo, CA: Primedia Enthusiasts Publications, 2004.

Estaville, Lawrence E., and Richard A. Earl. *Texas Water Atlas*. College Station: Texas A&M University Press, 2008.

Gordon, I. Herbert. *The Complete Book of Canoeing*. Guilford, CT: Globe Pequot Press, 2001.

Gorss, Jason, *High Performance Carbon Fibers*. Washington, DC: American Chemical Society, 2003.

Gould, F. W. *Texas Plants: A Checklist and Ecological Summary*. College Station: Texas A&M University Press, 1969.

Grant, Gordon. *Canoeing*. New York: W. W. Norton, 1997.

Gullion, Laurie. *Canoeing*. Champaign, IL: Human Kinetics Publishers, 1994.

———. *Canoeing and Kayaking*. Birmingham, AL: Menasha Ridge Press, 1987.

Harrison, Dave, ed. *Canoeing*. Mechanicsburg, PA: Stackpole Books, 1998.

Harte-Hanks Communications, Inc. "A Report by the Texas Poll." Austin, TX, July 1996.

Harte-Hanks Texas Poll. "A Report by the Texas Poll." Austin, TX: Harte Hanks Communications, June 17–27, 1996, 1–14.

Heed, Peter, and Dick Mansfield. *Canoe Racing*. Montpelier, VT: Vitesse Press, 2004.

Hodge, Larry D. *Official Guide to Texas Wildlife Management Areas*. Austin: Texas Parks and Wildlife Press, 2000.

Jacobson, Cliff. *Basic Essentials—Canoeing, a Falcon Guide*. Guilford, CT: Falcon, 2007.

Jennings, John, ed. *Bark Canoes*. Toronto: Firefly Books, 2012.

———. *The Canoe, a Living Tradition*. Toronto: Firefly Books, 2002.

Jones, Dilwyn. *Boats*. Austin: University of Texas Press, 1995.

Langley, Ricky L. "Alligator Attacks on Humans in the United States." *Wilderness and Environmental Medicine* 16 (2005): 118–24.

LaRoe, E. T., G. S. Farris, C. E. Puckett, P. D. Doran, and M. J. Mac, eds. "Our Living Resources: A Report to the Nation on the Distribution, Abundance, and Health of U.S. Plants, Animals, and Ecosystems." Washington, DC: US Department of the Interior, National Biological Service, 1995.

Lazarine, Paul. *Common Wetland Plants of Southeast Texas*. Galveston, TX: United States Army Corps of Engineers, 1981.

Loeffler, Cindy. "A Brief History of Environmental Flows in Texas." World and Environmental Resources Congress, Austin, TX, 2015, 2350–59.

Lower Colorado River Authority. *The Lower Colorado River Users Guide*. Austin, TX: Lower Colorado River Authority, 2001.

Mac, M. J., P. A. Opler., C. E. Puckett Haecker, and P. D. Doran, eds. *Status and Trends of the Nation's Biological Resources*, vols. 1 and 2. Washington, DC: US Department of Interior, US Geological Survey, 1998.

Marcee, Clarisa. "Sacred Springs." *Outdoor Magazine of Texas*, June 1999.

Mason, Bill. *Path of the Paddle*. Minocqua, WI: NorthWord Press, 1995.

McGuffin, Gary, and Joanie McGuffin. *Paddle Your Own Canoe*. Erin, ON: Boston Mill Press, 1999.

McKinney, Larry. "Water for the Future." *Outdoor Magazine of Texas*, July 2002.

Mitchell, Steve. "The Birth of Fiberglass Boats." *Good Old Boat* 2, no. 6 (1999). http://www.goodoldboat.com/reader_services/articles/birthoffiberglass.php.

Monk, Cark, and Jerome Knap. *A Complete Guide to Canoeing*. Toronto: Pagurian Press, 1976.

Moores, Ted. "From Forest to Factory." In *The Canoe, A Living Tradition*, by John Jennings, 162–193. Toronto: Firefly Books, 2002

National Parks Service. "The Grand Portage Guide, Grand Portage National Monument." Grand Portage, MN, 2014.

National Safe Boating Council. *Saved by the Jacket*. Delaware, OH: Personal Flotation Device Manufacturers Association, 2000.

National Safety Council. *Basic Life Support: Healthcare and Professional Rescuers*. New York: McGraw Hill, 2007.

Nolen, Ben, and Bob Narramore. *Rivers and Rapids*. Garland, TX: Ben Nolen and Bob Narramore, 1992.

Outdoor Foundation. *2015 Special Report on Paddlesports*. Washington, DC: Outdoor Foundation, 2015.

Peterson, Roger Troy. *A Field Guide to the Birds of Texas*. Boston: Houghton Mifflin, 1963.

Poling, Jim, Sr. *The Canoe: An Illustrated History*. Woodstock, VT: Countryman Press, 2000.

Ross, David. *Ships: Visual Encyclopedia*. New York: Chartwell Books, 2013.

Schmitz, D. C., B. V. Nelson, L. E. Nall, and J. D. Schardt. "Exotic Aquatic Plants in Florida: A Historical Perspective and Review of the Present Aquatic Plant Regulation Program." In "Proceedings of the Symposium on Exotic Pest Plants (Center, T. D., et al., eds.). Held on November 2–4, 1988, University of Miami, Rosentiel School of Martine and Atmospheric Science, Miami, Florida." Washington, DC: US Department of the Interior, National Park Service Document, 1991, 303–23.

Sibley, David Allen. *The Sibley Guide to Birds*. New York: Knopf, 2000.

Sitton, Thad. *Caddo: Visions of a Southern Cypress Lake*. College Station: Texas A&M University Press, 2015.

Sitton, Thad, and James Conrad, eds. *Every Sun That Rises: Wyatt Moore of Caddo Lake*. Austin: University of Texas Press, 1985.

Smith, Sonia, "Texas Waterways Are Nation's Fourth Most Polluted." *Texas Monthly*, January 21, 2013.

Spain, Bob. "Field Notes: Coastal Paddling Trails." *Texas Saltwater Fishing Magazine*, December 2007, 56 and 58.

Stockman, George. United States Canoeing Association, Lafayette, Indiana, 1993.

Stuhaug, Dennis O., and the Editors of Canoe and Kayak Magazine. *The Complete Idiots Guide to Canoeing and Kayaking*. New York: Alpha Books, 2004.

Texas Parks and Wildlife Department. "An Analysis of Texas Waterways." Texas Agricultural Extension Service and Texas Parks and Wildlife Department, Austin, TX, 1974.

———. "Natural Agenda: A Strategic Plan for Texas Parks and Wildlife Department." Austin, TX, 1993.

———. "Natural Agenda: A Strategic Plan for Texas Parks and Wildlife Department." Austin, TX, 2013.

———. "Renovated Matagorda Island Lighthouse." News release, Austin, TX, May 17, 2004.

———. "Seagrass Conservation Plan for Texas, 1999." Austin TX, 1999.

Texas Water Development Board. "Water for Texas." Austin, TX, 2012.

Tuttle, Merlin D. *Texas Bats*. Austin, TX: Bat Conservation International, 2003.

Tveten, John, and Gloria Tveten. *Wildflowers of Houston and Southeast Texas*. Austin: University of Texas Press, 1993.

US Department of the Interior—National Biological Services. *Our Living Resources*. Washington, DC: US Government Printing Office, 1995.

US Department of the Interior—US Geological Survey. *Status and Trends of the Nation's Biological Resources*, vols. 1 and 2. Washington, DC: US Government Printing Office, 1998.

US Geological Survey, National Weather System, Gauge 08167500. www.waterdata.usgs.gov/tx, 2011–16.

Warren, Graham, and David Gidmark. *Canoe Paddles*. Buffalo, NY: Firefly Books, 2004.

Wassenich, Dianne. "Springing to Life." In *The Living Waters of Texas*, edited by Ken Kramer and Charles Kruvand, 21–32. College Station: Texas A&M University Press, 2010.

Wilson, Anthony. *The Macmillan Visual Timeline of Transportation*. Macmillan Canada, 1995.

# Index

The letter *f* following a page number denotes a figure, the letter *m* denotes a map.